T0210496

Automated Software Diversity

Synthesis Lectures on Information Security, Privacy, & Trust

Editors
Elisa Bertino, *Purdue University*
Ravi Sandhu, *University of Texas at Austin*

The Synthesis Lectures Series on Information Security, Privacy, and Trust publishes 50- to 100-page publications on topics pertaining to all aspects of the theory and practice of Information Security, Privacy, and Trust. The scope largely follows the purview of premier computer security research journals such as ACM Transactions on Information and System Security, IEEE Transactions on Dependable and Secure Computing and Journal of Cryptology, and premier research conferences, such as ACM CCS, ACM SACMAT, ACM AsiaCCS, ACM CODASPY, IEEE Security and Privacy, IEEE Computer Security Foundations, ACSAC, ESORICS, Crypto, EuroCrypt and AsiaCrypt. In addition to the research topics typically covered in such journals and conferences, the series also solicits lectures on legal, policy, social, business, and economic issues addressed to a technical audience of scientists and engineers. Lectures on significant industry developments by leading practitioners are also solicited.

Automated Software Diversity
Per Larsen, Stefan Brunthaler, Lucas Davi, Ahmad-Reza Sadeghi, and Michael Franz
2015

Trust in Social Media
Jiliang Tang and Huan Liu
2015

Physically Unclonable Functions (PUFs): Applications, Models, and Future Directions
Christian Wachsmann and Ahmad-Reza Sadeghi
2014

Usable Security: History, Themes, and Challenges
Simson Garfinkel and Heather Richter Lipford
2014

Automated Software Diversity

Per Larsen, Stefan Brunthaler, Lucas Davi, Ahmad-Reza Sadeghi, and Michael Franz

ISBN: 978-3-031-01218-1   paperback
ISBN: 978-3-031-02346-0   ebook

DOI 10.1007/978-3-031-02346-0

A Publication in the Springer series
SYNTHESIS LECTURES ON INFORMATION SECURITY, PRIVACY, & TRUST

Lecture #14
Series Editors: Elisa Bertino, *Purdue University*
                Ravi Sandhu, *University of Texas at Austin*
Series ISSN
Print 1945-9742   Electronic 1945-9750

Automated Software Diversity

Per Larsen
Immunant, Inc., USA

Stefan Brunthaler
SBA Research, Vienna, Austria

Lucas Davi
Technische Universität Darmstadt, Germany

Ahmad-Reza Sadeghi
Technische Universität Darmstadt, Germany

Michael Franz
University of California, Irvine, USA

SYNTHESIS LECTURES ON INFORMATION SECURITY, PRIVACY, & TRUST #14

ABSTRACT

Whereas user-facing applications are often written in modern languages, the firmware, operating system, support libraries, and virtual machines that underpin just about any modern computer system are still written in low-level languages that value flexibility and performance over convenience and safety. Programming errors in low-level code are often exploitable and can, in the worst case, give adversaries unfettered access to the compromised host system.

This book provides an introduction to and overview of automatic software diversity techniques that, in one way or another, use randomization to greatly increase the difficulty of exploiting the vast amounts of low-level code in existence. Diversity-based defenses are motivated by the observation that a single attack will fail against multiple targets with unique attack surfaces. We introduce the many, often complementary, ways that one can diversify attack surfaces and provide an accessible guide to more than two decades worth of research on the topic. We also discuss techniques used in conjunction with diversity to prevent accidental disclosure of randomized program aspects and present an in-depth case study of one of our own diversification solutions.

KEYWORDS

software diversity, code randomization, data randomization, information leaks, leakage resilience, code reuse, exploitation

Contents

Preface

To err is human or so the Latin proverb goes. In spite of all technological progress since classical antiquity, human error has not been eliminated. While computer programmers have numerous tools at their disposal to help catch and correct mistakes, modern software development is so complex that residual errors inevitably remain as programs are released to end users. This is a book about the security implications of some such errors and a family of techniques—collectively known as software diversity—that prevent reliable exploitation of software flaws by making the target environment less predictable for an attacker.

Per Larsen, Stefan Brunthaler, Lucas Davi, Ahmad-Reza Sadeghi, and Michael Franz
December 2015

Acknowledgments

The authors thank Andrei Homescu, Stephen Crane, Todd Jackson, Steven Neisius, and Alen Stojanov for their contributions to the work presented in this book. Hamed Okhravi and Mathias Payer provided lots of constructive suggestions and feedback on draft manuscripts; thank you!

This material is based upon work partially supported by the Defense Advanced Research Projects Agency (DARPA) under contracts D11PC20024, N660001-1-2-4014, FA8750-15-C-0124, FA8750-15-C-0085, and N66001-13-C-4057 as well as gifts from Mozilla, Oracle, and Qualcomm. Any opinions, findings, and conclusions or recommendations expressed in this material are those of the authors and do not necessarily reflect the views of the Defense Advanced Research Projects Agency (DARPA), its Contracting Agents, or any other agency of the U.S. Government.

Portions of this work are from Larsen et al. [76], copyright © 2014, IEEE.

Portions of this work are from Crane et al. [39], copyright © 2015, IEEE.

Portions of this work are from Homescu et al. [61], copyright © 2015, IEEE.

Per Larsen, Stefan Brunthaler, Lucas Davi, Ahmad-Reza Sadeghi, and Michael Franz
December 2015

CHAPTER 1

Introduction

In countless literary and real-life "bank heist" stories, the plot revolves around a group of perpetrators digging an underground tunnel to the bank's vault, or breaking through the wall of an adjoining building, thereby circumventing the physical security (walls, doors, locks) that the bank has put in place to safeguard its treasures. Many of these plot lines revolve around a blueprint of the bank building, which exposes a weakness of the bank's defenses that only the criminals know about, and which is critical to the success of the criminals' plan.

While analogies with the physical world are of course imperfect, many cyber attacks proceed in surprisingly similar ways to such bank heists: the attacker uses an information advantage about a vulnerability as a blueprint to breach a weakness in software that is unknown to the software's designers and users. Just as in the tunneling bank heist, the attacker is not coming through the well-fortified front door at all, but sneakily drilling through a deficient wall or floor.

A problem with software that doesn't exist with banks is that a lot of computers are running the exact same software, which all have the exact same blueprint and hence identical vulnerabilities. While finding a flaw in a blueprint in the physical world will give a team of villains the capability to break into precisely that one particular bank vault, finding a software flaw in the cyber world might give a cyber villain the capability to break into *all* copies of that software—potentially running on hundreds of millions of computers.

This book is about techniques to vary the "blueprints" of different copies of the same software, and then hiding them from potential attackers. The first feature greatly reduces the chance that an attack that works on one copy of a software program will also work on all other copies of the same program. The second makes it more difficult for attackers to spy out the actual blueprint of any particular piece of software running on a specific computer. In concert, these two techniques significantly raise the bar for cyber attackers.

In the following, when we speak about "hiding" the blueprints (i.e., the implementation details) of software, we do not mean cryptography. While programs can in principle be encrypted just like any other data, they would need to be decrypted prior to execution. On current commodity hardware, this would add significant computational overhead. We will focus instead on techniques that are practically deployable today on commercial off-the-shelf hardware.

When we vary the blueprints of software from one version to the next, we create what is called artificial or automated software diversity (automated, as opposed to manual, requiring the intervention of a human programmer, which is costly). Conceptually, this randomization process takes an input program representation and produces an output program representation in which implementation aspects such as the code layout have changed. Rather than being perfect copies of one another, randomizing programs in this manner causes the program implementations to diverge, in a manner that is hopefully not predictable by an attacker.

The key idea behind software diversity, also known as code randomization, is that if there is a flaw in the program, the randomization process affects the location or representation of the flaw so it becomes harder if not impossible to exploit it. To attain this goal, we need to do more than just randomize programs: we also need to ensure that the attacker cannot use information leakage or probing to find flaws *after* we have randomized them.

Beyond providing randomization and hiding the results of the randomization, a diversifying defense also needs to avoid interfering with the users and developers of the protected programs. To remain transparent to users, software diversity must not cause programs to run noticeably slower nor must it affect the intended functionality of the program. To remain transparent to software developers, diversity must not interfere with the way software is built, distributed, updated, and maintained. Taken together, this is a high bar to meet, and perhaps the reason why only one diversification technique [95] has seen widespread adoption so far. It is the goal of this book to cover the many aspects of software diversity in a cohesive framework that serves as a guide and entry point to the substantial academic literature relating to, in one way or another, software diversity.

1.1   A BRIEF HISTORY OF PROGRAM RANDOMIZATION

The idea of software diversity was originally explored as a way to obtain fault-tolerance in mission critical software. Approaches to software fault-tolerance are broadly classified as single-version or multi-version techniques. Early examples of the latter kind include Recovery Blocks [100] and N-Version programming [5] that introduce diversity manually.

The idea of automatic software diversity (or program evolution) was first introduced by Cohen [28] in his seminal work on how to protect computer systems and the programs they were running. His basic observation was that an adversary typically generates an attack vector and aims to simultaneously compromise as many systems as possible using the same attack vector. To mitigate this so-called ultimate attack, Cohen proposed to diversify a software program into multiple and different instances while each instance implements the programmer-intended functionality.

To quote Cohen:

> The ultimate defense is to drive the complexity of the ultimate attack up so high that the cost of attack is too high to be worth performing. [...], even though it could eventually be successful.

Cohen's description of the ultimate attack and ultimate defense still hold two decades after publication, as does his recount of attacker economics. In fact, we share his assessment that diversity makes certain attacks economically unviable and can eliminate certain attacks altogether.

In 1997, Forrest et al. [49] described the first (to the best of our knowledge) practical implementation of a system that uses software diversity as a security defense, implementing or discussing several of Cohen's ideas. Forrest's work focuses on stack-based buffer overflows but also introduces some other diversifying code transformations (basic block reordering, randomized instruction scheduling) that are now becoming increasingly important, due to their ability to thwart code-reuse attacks [87, 110]. Their experimental results show that software diversity can be practical and efficient, encouraging all later work on software diversity.

One of the most popular instantiations of a software diversity scheme is randomization of the application's memory layout: address space layout randomization (ASLR) varies the base address of code and data segments each time an application is run. Hence, the locations of the memory fragments that the adversary uses in his exploit are not known *a priori*. Today, ASLR is enabled on nearly all modern operating systems including Windows, Linux, OS X, iOS, and Android. For the most part, current ASLR schemes randomize the base (start) address of segments such as the stack, heap, libraries, and the executable itself. This book covers many schemes that improve upon this basic approach.

In 2010, Franz [50] anticipated lasting changes in the software world that make it possible to bring automated software diversity to the people *without* them actually noticing. Franz described a paradigm shift in software delivery: instead of using physical media in shrink-wrapped boxes, the world is moving toward an environment in which almost all software is delivered electronically from "App Stores" or similar online software delivery mechanisms. The shift from physical to virtual delivery of software makes it possible to supply each user with a different binary.

Although software delivery via physical media is all but gone, the delivery mechanisms that replaced them are typically built around the assumption that all users will receive a clone of the "golden master" version of a given software release. Provisioning, checksumming, caching, and patching mechanisms make the same assumption tacitly. At first, this may seem to put diversity at an inherent disadvantage relative to other exploit mitigation and software protection mechanisms. However, diversification need not happen at the factory. Instead, one may opt to perform randomization when the program is loaded [43, 82, 123] or during execution [12, 53]. Forrest observed that load-time diversification "is likely to be less expensive" and thus more practical than compile-time diversification which in turn is less expensive than manually developing multiple versions of the same program. In fact, ASLR relies mainly on load-time randomization and we believe that any improved schemes aiming to be immediately useful must follow the same model.

1.2   BOOK OVERVIEW

The book is structured around a series of questions. The first question—"what attacks are we concerned with?"—is addressed in our background chapter on attacks and defenses. Readers with substantial knowledge in information security can safely skip to the third chapter which asks "what to diversify?" We ask "when to diversify?" in Chapter 4 and explain the various times in the software life cycle that one can apply software diversity techniques. Chapter 5 seeks to answer the question "how to diversify?" by providing a detailed case study of one particular diversification approach. The last two chapters are devoted to advanced topics. Chapter 6 provides an overview of techniques that seek to ensure that the results of the diversification process remain hidden even when the adversary can disclose the memory contents of a victim program. Finally, Chapter 7 briefly describes concerns relevant to research and development of advanced software diversity techniques.

CHAPTER 2

Attacking and Defending

Attackers and defenders in cyberspace engage in a continuous arms race. As new attacks appear, new defenses are created in response—leading to increased complexity in both cases. To motivate a study of software diversity, we briefly summarize the evolution and current state of computer security.

2.1 TAXONOMY OF ATTACKS

There is a large spectrum of attacks that an attacker can use against a target, employing a wide range of low-level techniques. Figure 2.1 provides a high-level overview of the most prominent attack techniques leveraged against computing platforms ranging from low-level hardware attacks, attacks against the operating system kernel [63], up to attacks that target the application layer [3, 17, 18, 87, 105, 111, 113]. Since software diversity aims at mitigating attacks on the application and the operating system layer, we focus in this book on attacks that target these layers, i.e., attacks A to C in Figure 2.1.

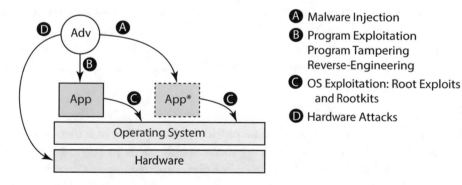

Figure 2.1: Threat landscape.

A prevalent attack vector against today's systems is malware injection (A). The main idea behind such an attack is the construction of a self-contained malicious application that is downloaded and installed on the victim's PC platform. However, one of the challenges for malware injection is the distribution of the malware. For instance, an attacker needs to fool the user to download the malware. Further, when the malware is to be uploaded on an application market, the attacker needs to undermine the application vetting process. In contrast, exploiting existing benign software programs (B) only requires the adversary to exploit a program bug in one of the existing applications running on the victim's PC. A prominent target for such attacks are web browsers, document viewers, or Word processors, as these programs continuously suffer from program bugs. Apart from exploiting program bugs, attackers often seek to learn the application's internal behavior by means of reverse-engineering, or modify existing applications to embed new malicious code. The former is often performed to discover program vulnerabilities, identify and leak application secrets, or simply to learn the programming techniques for a given task.

It should be noted that both exploitation of existing benign apps as well as injecting malicious applications can serve as an entry point to launch more sophisticated attacks that target the underlying operating system kernel (C). These attacks are particularly dangerous as they eventually allow the attacker to control the entire system to arbitrarily change its behavior, and leak private information.

As we will show throughout this book, software diversity techniques aid in mitigating all the attacks from A to C. However, the research community has mainly focused on leveraging software diversity as a defense against program exploitation. As a consequence, we will thoroughly describe software diversity techniques against this class of attacks, and only provide short discussions of defenses that aim at preventing malware injection and attacks against the operating system kernel.

In the following, we present more details on the attacks that are most relevant to automated software diversity.

2.1.1   MEMORY CORRUPTION ATTACKS

The attacker often needs to modify the internal program state located in memory. This can be either the end-goal of the attack or an intermediate step (for example, an attacker may seek to modify a function pointer to hijack program control flow). This class covers a large variety of techniques that use programming errors to achieve the same goal: changing the memory contents of the target program [115].

Buffer Overflows   Buffer overflows are a popular instantiation of memory corruption attacks. In a buffer overflow, the attacker writes data outside of the bounds of a memory buffer to corrupt memory adjacent to that buffer. This approach is only viable in languages such as Fortran, C, and C++ which eschew bounds checking out of performance concerns. Stack smashing [3] is a commonly used technique in which a stack-based buffer overflow is used to overwrite the return address stored in an adjacent stack location. Heap-based buffer overflows are also useful to adversaries.

Attack Flavors   An overview of the different flavors of memory corruption attacks is shown in Figure 2.2. Typically, every memory corruption attack involves altering of program data (A). A well-known target is the program's stack and heap which contain return addresses and function pointers. Once an attacker can manipulate these data fields, she can redirect execution to unintended code sequence residing in the same address space. For instance, a conventional mem-

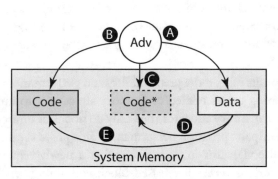

Figure 2.2: Overview of memory corruption attacks.

ory corruption attack on the stack [3] involves injection of malicious code into memory (C), overwriting a function's return address (A) which leads to an unintended control-flow redirection to attacker's injected code (D). Alternatively, an attacker can exploit a memory corruption vulnerability to maliciously combine already existing, benign code to induce malicious program actions (E). These so-called code-reuse attacks are challenging to prevent as they leverage benign code [74, 87, 101]. Another attack strategy is to modify existing code in memory (B). Such attacks are not as prevalent today since code memory is typically marked as non-writable. Lastly, an attacker can exploit a memory corruption vulnerability to learn and leak the code and data memory in attack (A) and (B). For instance, memory disclosure can be leveraged to undermine memory randomization as discussed in the following section.

2.1.2 INFORMATION LEAKS

Often, the attacker seeks to read some sensitive program state. This includes contents of processor registers, memory pages, process meta-data, files, etc. Such information can be valuable to an attacker by itself (e.g., credit card numbers, login credentials, or other personal user information) or to further an on-going attack (by locating protected objects in memory through a pointer leak, or by reading encryption keys used to encrypt other data). In general, information leaks are increasingly used to overcome situations where attackers lack knowledge of program internals [13, 108, 109, 113, 114]. For example, information leaks help bypass address space layout randomization in later stages of an attack [102]. Chapter 6 provides an in-depth discussion of information leakage and memory leakage defenses in context of automated software diversity.

Side Channel Attacks   We consider side channel attacks as a category of information leaks. Whereas most other information leaks are intrusive (using some exploit to explicitly reveal program data in unintended ways), side channel attacks infer internal program state in a black box manner by analyzing the interactions between the program and its outside environment. One common measurement used by these attacks is timing [73]; the attacker measures how the time between externally visible program events changes in response to some stimulus applied by the attacker, and if the response is also correlated with the value of some internal program variable. Many types of stimuli are available to an attacker, such as memory or cache pressure [119, 126].

Memory Allocator Exploits   Such exploits rely on the predictability and performance constraints of memory allocators, or on programming errors related to memory allocation, to implement a memory corruption attack. For example, memory allocators typically do not clear unused memory after de-allocation requests, because it impairs program performance. This poses significant security problems. Attackers manipulate the allocator in such a way that a newly requested block (under the control of the attacker) overlaps recently released block containing sensitive data. Memory-management errors in applications are also a significant threat; one example is use-after-free errors, where the attacker uses a stale pointer to deallocated memory to read or write a newly allocated block that overlaps the deallocated block.

2.1.3   CODE INJECTION

Another way of exploiting a program is to make it execute code under the attacker's control, potentially leading to the attacker taking control of the entire program or even system (programs running with administrator privileges effectively control the entire machine). To achieve this, the attacker injects malicious code into a running program and then redirects execution to the injected code [3]. This attack requires (i) a memory corruption vulnerability, (ii) an executable and writable region of memory, and (iii) a way to direct the processor to execute newly written data. The third requirement is usually met through memory corruption as well, by modifying a code pointer (like the on-stack return address) to point to the new code. The attacker then crafts a native code payload, writes it to memory, then redirects execution to it. The processor executes the newly inserted block, leaving the attacker in control of the thread of execution.

2.1.4   CODE REUSE

Operating systems used to allow execution of most program data. This enabled code injection. For example, the entire native stack was executable on Windows and Linux systems. To prevent code injection attacks, operating systems now implement a security model (known as Data Execution Prevention—DEP—or W⊕X [95]) which mandates that a memory page is either writable or executable, but not both at the same time. Code-reuse attacks [74, 87, 101, 118] have emerged as a new bypass to non-executable data defenses. Instead of injecting new code, attackers construct an attack from pieces of executable code. In the classic code-reuse attack, called return-into-libc, RILC, the attacker leverages dangerous library functions [87, 118]. A more generic code-reuse attack is return-oriented programming [101]. Instead of leveraging entire functions, the attacker only combines short instruction sequences (gadgets) from various library functions to generate arbitrary malicious program actions. At the time of writing this book, return-oriented programming has become the state-of-the-art exploitation technique to compromise modern software programs.

To address the emerging threat of code-reuse attacks, a number of new defenses have emerged of which some leverage software diversity techniques. However, many of the proposed defenses only tackle conventional return-oriented programming attacks, but do not prevent function-reuse attacks such as return-into-libc. Contrary to popular belief, these attacks are highly dangerous. Tran et al. [118] have shown that the functions residing in the standard UNIX C library libc form a Turing-complete language. The counterfeit object-oriented programming technique, COOP [40, 105], goes one step further and demonstrates that adversaries can generate arbitrary malicious program behavior by invoking a chain of C++ virtual methods.

In response to diversifying defenses, information leaks have become an increasingly crucial part of code-reuse attacks. One example of this development is a new code-reuse attack called just-in-time code reuse or JIT-ROP [113]. This attack demonstrates that leakage of a single run-time address (e.g., the address of a function pointer) can be exploited to disclose the randomized content of hundreds of memory pages. For this, JIT-ROP leverages a scripting engine such as Javascript to determine the start and end address of the memory page the initial leaked code pointer references. This is possible because contemporary PC platforms align memory pages to a boundary of 4KB. Once the start address of a memory page is known, the attacker can leverage the scripting engine to read and disassemble the page, and search for useful return-oriented gadgets. With very high probability the disclosed memory page will include references to other pages via direct call and jump instructions. As a consequence, the attacker can follow these references to disclose more code pages and gadgets. After collecting all gadgets, the attack code (containing a built-in gadget compiler) compiles a tailored code-reuse payload for that particular program and then runs the attack against the program.

2.1.5   JIT ATTACKS

The introduction of new programming models can change the landscape and introduce new threats to security. In recent years, just-in-time, JIT, compiled languages (such as Java and JavaScript) have become increasingly popular. For example, many dynamically generated or interactive web pages are written in JavaScript, and all major web browsers contain a JIT compiler for JavaScript. These languages allow programmers to create and run new code dynamically (during program execution); a JIT compiler then translates from source to binary code. This creates a new problem: the attacker can craft and insert malicious source code into the program itself. This is a variant of code injection applied to source code. Program source code is stored as non-executable data, so existing anti-code injection defenses are insufficient. JIT spraying [14] is a recent attack of this kind. When compiling expressions containing constant values, just-in-time compilers may embed the constants directly in binary code. This gives the attacker a way to inject arbitrary binary code into the program, by using constants that contain an attack payload.

2.1.6   PROGRAM TAMPERING

The ability to modify a program's state (tamper with the program) has many applications: the attacker can modify unprotected code pointers or instructions to execute arbitrary code, change program data to gain some benefit or bypass DRM protections. One example is bypassing checks in programs that prompt for passwords or serial numbers. Another example of tampering is cheating at computer games, where players give themselves unfair advantages by removing restrictions from the game. Tampering with a program may require the use of one or more of the previously described attacks, as intermediate steps to achieving the desired effect on the target.

Client-side tampering requires unfettered access to the target program, and the attacker is often also in control of the entire physical machine, as well as the operating system, running the program (this model is known as *man-at-the-end*, or MATE [31]). This is a different adversarial model from the other attacks, where the attacker has restricted access to the program, and little or no access to the underlying system.

2.1.7   REVERSE ENGINEERING

Often, the attacker seeks not to impact the execution of a program, but to find out how the program works internally. Notable uses include reimplementation, compatibility with new software, and defeating security-through-obscurity. Security researchers working on both offenses and defenses use reverse engineering to discover exploitable program vulnerabilities, both from the original program and from patches [34, 44].

2.2   TAXONOMY OF DEFENSES

Many attacks rely on program bugs that are fixable when the program source code is available. If this is not the case, or if attacks rely on intended program behavior, alternative techniques are available. We separate these techniques into the following categories:

2.2.1   ENFORCEMENT-BASED DEFENSES

To defend against attacks, some defenses seek to disallow behaviors required to mount an attack against a vulnerable program. Examples include checking the bounds on array accesses (against buffer overflows), making the data sections non-executable (against code injection) and restricting control-flow transfers to a set of pre-determined edges (to prevent control-flow hijacking and code-reuse attacks)—also known as Control-Flow Integrity (CFI) [1]. Software-Fault Isolation (SFI) [81, 120, 127] is a similar approach that confines the control flow and data accesses to a sandbox area. Code-Pointer Integrity (CPI) [75] is an enforcement-based technique that isolates pointers and other sensitive values as well pointers to sensitive values. Strong implementations of CPI use hardware or software fault isolation to protect all sensitive values [47]. Defenders can deploy these techniques during ahead-of-time compilation [45, 90, 116], during just-in-time compilation [91, 127], or through static binary rewriting [122, 128, 129] and dynamic binary rewriting [72, 97].

Due to the rise of code injection attacks, modern operating systems (Windows, Linux,[1] and OS X) all deploy one low-cost enforcement defense: Data Execution Prevention (DEP, also known as W⊕X). DEP requires the operating system to map all pages containing program data (such as the heap and stack) as non-executable, and all pages of program code as non-writable. This defense has negligible performance costs and effectively stopped most code injection attacks without requiring substantial changes to programs.

Other enforcement techniques require significant changes to protected programs and impose extra restrictions and costs on both programs and programmers. For example, array bounds checking requires extra operations around each array element access; CFI requires extra address checks around each indirect branch. In programs that contain many array accesses or indirect branches, these checks incur significant performance penalties. In addition, programmers have to account for the extra restrictions; for example, they must check that the program does not violate any security restriction during normal program operation. Therefore, we regard this class of defenses as the most intrusive.

2.2.2 PROGRAM INTEGRITY MONITORS

If an attack cannot be prevented, the last line of defense is stopping the program before the attacker has a chance to do any damage. Doing this manually requires significant effort and attention from program users. To stop the program, they first have to detect any unusual behavior in the operation of the program. In many cases, this unusual behavior is either invisible to the user, or is intentionally hidden by the attacker (to prevent detection). While defining when a program is acting "unusually" is very hard, detecting specific attacks is much simpler and can be easily automated in many cases. For each detectable attack, an integrity monitor periodically investigates the state of the running program and checks for signs of an attack.

Examples of such defenses are "stack canaries" [36], "heap canaries" [89], and various ROP detectors [25, 51, 94]. Code execution attacks often use buffer overflows to overwrite a code pointer, e.g., the return address of the currently executing function. To defend against this attack, modern compilers can insert canaries to guard the return address against changes by pairing it with a randomized guard value—the "canary." Any change to the return address will also change the canary, and the attacker cannot reasonably predict the random value of the canary. On every function return, the program checks the canary against the expected random value and terminates on mismatches. The overheads from the added checks are often negligible (less than 1% on average [115]).

Monitoring defenses are the least intrusive form of defense (in many cases, they can be deployed transparently to the program), but are the most vulnerable to detection and deception.

---

[1]The PaX Team implemented DEP on Linux [95].

Monitoring allows attackers the same amount of control as long as they remain undetected and they may detect and tamper with the monitor to let the attack succeed [20, 41, 55, 104].

2.2.3 DIVERSITY-BASED DEFENSES

Attackers often rely on being able to predict certain details of program implementation, such as the memory locations of sensitive program objects (like code pointers). Removing predictability is, in most cases, as effective as restricting what the attacker can do with the predicted knowledge. Diversification makes program implementations diverge between each computer system or between each execution. This means that the attacker has to either limit the attack to a small subset of predictable targets, or adjust the attack to account for diversity. The latter is impractical in most cases (because it would require duplicated attack effort for each different version of the target), so the malicious effects of the attacks are limited at worst to a small number of targets (where the attacker still gets full control, in absence of any monitoring or enforcement-based defenses).

The three following sections treat approaches to diversity in much greater detail. Researchers have investigated the practical uses of automated software diversity against the attacks enumerated in Section 2.1 (except information leaks and side channels). Figure 3.7 links attacks to corresponding studies of diversity.

2.2.4 PROGRAM OBFUSCATION

Obfuscation to prevent reverse engineering attacks [29, 30] is closely related to diversity and relies on many of the same code transformations. Diversity requires that program implementations are kept private and that implementations differ among systems; this is not required for obfuscation. Pucella and Schneider perform a comparative analysis of obfuscation, diversification, and type systems within a single semantic framework [99].

CHAPTER 3

What to Diversify

At the core of any approach to software diversity, whether performed manually by programmers or automatically by a compiler or binary rewriter, is a set of randomizing transformations that make functionally equivalent program copies diverge. A second distinguishing factor among approaches is when diversity is introduced in the software life cycle. These two choices—*what* to diversify and *when* to diversify—constitute the major axes of the design space and together determine the fundamental properties of any concrete approach. This chapter focuses on the former choice and Chapter 4 addresses the latter.

Randomizing transformations are conceptually similar to compiler optimizations. Both consist of three steps: (i) determining if a code fragment can be transformed, (ii) estimating if the transformation is profitable, and (iii) applying the transformation. A diversifying transformation differs in the second step by adding an element of chance. The heuristic that determines whether to transform a code fragment or not is replaced (or extended) with a random choice using a pseudo-random number generator (PRNG). Early studies of security via software diversity were compiler-based [28, 49].

Like compiler optimizations, the scope of diversifying transformations varies in their scope (or granularity) from single instructions all the way up to the entirety of the program. The following sections present diversifying transformations in ascending order of scope.

3.1 INSTRUCTION LEVEL

These transformations affect at most a few instructions inside a single basic block.[1]. Displacing a sequence of instructions breaks fine-grained code-reuse attacks (assuming implementation details do not leak to attackers as we will explain in Chapter 6). They include but are not limited to:

Equivalent Instruction Substitution   The functionality of some instructions overlaps with that of others such that it is often possible to substitute one for another [46, 61, 69]. Load instructions that support multiple addressing modes are common examples (see Figure 3.1).

Equivalent Instruction Sequences   Substituting one or more instructions for another instruction sequence leads to even more randomization opportunities. For instance, negation followed by subtraction can substitute for integer addition.

---

[1]A basic block is an instruction sequence that executes atomically as a unit or not at all as explained in Section 3.2.

Instruction Reordering   It is well known that instructions can execute in any order that preserves the dependencies between data-producing and data-consuming instructions. Using a compiler's instruction scheduler to randomize the instruction order increases diversity among the output binaries (see Figure 3.2) [61].

Register Allocation Randomization   While program performance is highly dependent on what variables are allocated to registers, the particular register a variable is assigned to is often irrelevant. Consequently, it is straightforward to randomize register assignments (see Figure 3.3) [16, 39, 61, 93]. Register spilling and re-materialization heuristics are amenable to randomization, too.

Garbage Code Insertion   This transformation can be as simple as adding no-operation instructions (NOPs, see Figure 3.4), or as complex as inserting entirely new statements. In contrast to many other transformations, garbage insertion is always possible and hence allows production of infinitely many program variants.

3.2   BASIC BLOCK LEVEL

A basic block is a sequence of instructions that are executed atomically. Therefore, branch instructions can only appear as the last instruction in a basic block; basic blocks without a terminating branch simply fall through to the successor block [117]. The following transformations diversify basic blocks:

Basic Block Shuffling   Basic blocks can be laid out in any randomly chosen order. Shuffling of basic blocks may require insertion of additional jumps between pairs of basic blocks chained together on fall-through paths (i.e., without branches) and make branches between blocks that are contiguous after randomization superfluous. Basic blocks can be randomized inside each individual function or method [49, 82, 123] or at the module level by interspersing basic blocks from different functions. Basic blocks that are chained through sequences of fall-through paths can be treated as a unit during shuffling to lower the performance impact [33]. Basic block splitting and merging creates additional reordering opportunities.

Opaque Predicate Insertion   A single-predecessor block b can be substituted with a conditional branch to b and its clone b' using an arbitrary predicate [29, 30]. These predicates can also guard blocks of garbage code so they never execute.

Branch Function Insertion   Branch functions do not return to their callers; instead, they contain code that determines the return address based on the call site [78]. Branch functions can replace direct control transfers via branches and fall-through paths. Similarly, direct calls to functions can be replaced by call functions that obfuscate the call graph.

Control Flow Flattening   Finally, the topology of a function's control-flow graph can be obscured by replacing direct jumps connecting basic blocks with indirect jumps that go through "jump

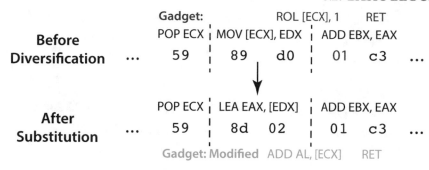

Figure 3.1: Effect of substituting equivalent instructions.

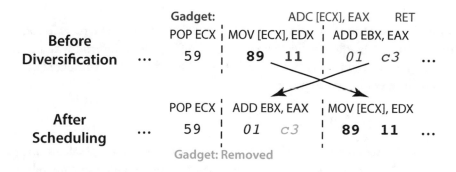

Figure 3.2: Effect of reordering instructions by changing instruction schedule.

Figure 3.3: Effect of register allocation randomizing.

tables" [28, 121]. After flattening, all basic blocks inside a function have a common predecessor and successor block. A special variable is introduced so that a basic block can specify which of the original basic blocks should execute next.

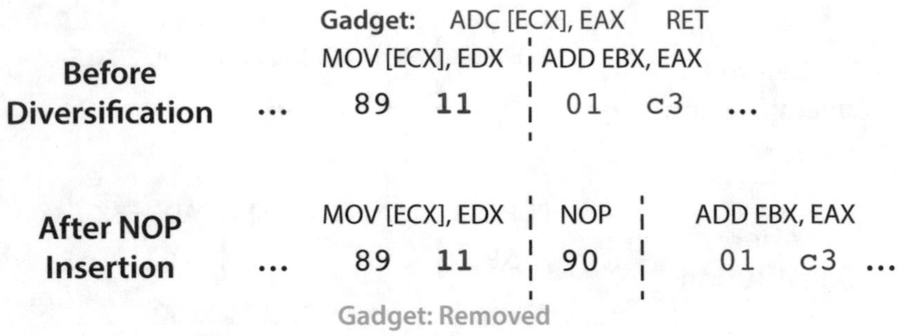

	Gadget:	ADC [ECX], EAX	RET
Before Diversification	MOV [ECX], EDX	ADD EBX, EAX	
···	89 11	01 c3 ···	

	MOV [ECX], EDX	NOP	ADD EBX, EAX
After NOP Insertion ···	89 11	90	01 c3 ···

Gadget: Removed

Figure 3.4: Effect of inserting no op (NOP) instructions in between two regularly emitted instructions.

All basic block transformations affect the code layout and make reliable code reuse attacks harder to construct. Opaque predicate insertion, branch function insertion, and control flow flattening make reverse engineering harder and also make it difficult to correlate two closely related binaries to reverse engineer patches [33].

3.3   LOOP LEVEL

Forrest et al. [49] proposes diversifying transformations focusing on parallelizable blocks, which includes but is not restricted to loops. The proposed techniques are, unfortunately, not evaluated.

3.4   FUNCTION LEVEL

Transformations at this granularity include:

Stack Layout Randomization   Using a buffer overflow to overwrite the return address stored on the machine stack on x86 processors is a classic attack vector. As a result, many randomizing transformations target the stack, including:

- stack frame padding (see Figure 3.5) [11, 49],

- stack variable reordering (see Figure 3.5) [11, 49],

- stack growth reversal [67], and

- non-contiguous stack allocation [24, 49].

The last transformation allocates a callee stack frame at a randomly chosen location rather than a location adjacent to the stack frame of the calling function. A concrete implementation of this idea is provided by StackArmor [24]. By way of implementing the idea of a non-contiguous growing stack, StackArmor proposes additional ideas not presented by Forrest et al. [49]. For

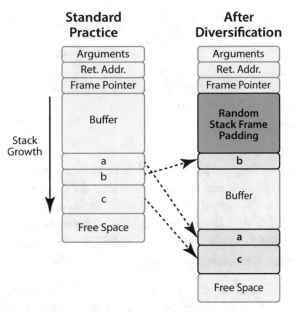

Figure 3.5: Effect of stack layout randomization. Arrows indicate stack variable reordering.

example, StackArmor implements a technique to ensure that repeated function-call stack frames will be put on random addresses. As a result, the attacker cannot use temporal observation of repeated function calls to his advantage.

Function Parameter Randomization   This transformation permutes the existing formal parameters and may add new ones as long as all call-sites can be rewritten to match the actual parameters with the modified formal parameters [31]. This transformation is employed against tampering, code matching, and return-into-libc attacks.

Inlining, Outlining, and Splitting   Inlining the target of a function call into the call-site is a well known compiler optimization. Function outlining is the inverse of inlining: it extracts one or more basic blocks and encapsulates them in their own subroutine. As a special case of function outlining, a function may be split into two; all live variables at the point of the split are passed as parameters to the second function. Together, these transformations randomize the number of function calls and the amount of code duplication among program variants to prevent code matching.

3.5   PROGRAM LEVEL

Transformations at this level include the following.

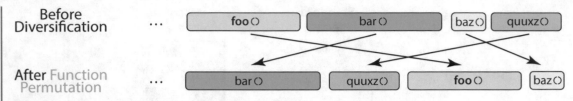

Figure 3.6: Function permutation.

Base Address Randomization, ASLR It used to be the case that the base of the code and data segments (i.e., the stack, heap, and statically allocated data) were always loaded at fixed virtual memory addresses. Since the virtual address space of each process is private, the starting address can be chosen at random. ASLR implements base address randomization and is currently the only deployed probabilistic defense [10, 15, 95]. ASLR complicates memory corruption, code injection, and code reuse attacks, but can be bypassed via information leaks [13, 113].

Function Reordering Functions can be laid out in any order within executables and libraries (see Figure 3.6) [16, 39, 71, 123]. For dynamically linked functions, the tables maintained by the dynamic linker (e.g., the GOT and PLT dynamic linking structures on Linux systems) can be randomized, too.

Program Encoding Randomization It is possible to substitute one encoding of a program for another as long as there is a way to reverse the process. The encoding is reversed by a virtual machine that either interprets the randomized instructions, or emulates a machine for the randomized encoding by translating fragments back to native code prior to execution. Many types of encodings can be used for this purpose. For instance, one of the simplest and fastest encodings computes the exclusive-or of the original program bytes and a randomly chosen key; applying the same transformation when the instructions are about to execute recovers the original encoding. This approach is known as *Instruction Set Randomization* [7, 70]. More complex encodings may compress the instruction stream or offer stronger encryption guarantees. Some encodings are designed to randomize the code layout [57] or code addresses [112]. These transformations can defend against both code injection and fine-grained code reuse attacks.

Data Randomization These transformations aim to stop memory corruption attacks with the exception of constant blinding which defends against JIT-spraying. Several variations are possible:

- *Data Randomization.* The representation of data can be randomized, for example, by XOR-ing every data value with a randomly choosen bitmask [9, 19]. Key to this approach is to separate objects into a number of equivalence classes based on aliasing relations and XOR objects in each equivalence class with a different key. Points-to analysis computes aliasing relations under the assumption that all objects are accessed correctly, i.e., in the absence of memory corruption. This is precisely the assumption that adversaries violate: they may use an overflown array to access objects in other equivalence classes such as scalars and return addresses. With XOR "encryption" of data values, malicious memory accesses are likely to lead to a mismatch between the bitmasks used to load and store values and thus foil the attacker.

- *Static Data Randomization.* The layout of static variables can be permuted and padding can be added via dummy variables [11, 28, 49].

- *Constant Blinding.* A constant c is blinded by applying an injective function $f(c, x) = c'$ where x is a randomly chosen value. During execution, c is obtained by computing $f^{-1}(c', x)$. The exclusive-or operation is a common choice for f and f^{-1}.

- *Structure Layout Randomization.* Composite data structures such as classes and `structs` can have their layout randomized similarly to static data randomization [23, 53, 77].

- *Heap Layout Randomization.* The layout of dynamically allocated objects can be randomized by adding random padding to each object [10, 92]. The memory allocator can also split the heap into multiple regions and pick a region in which to store each object at random.

Library Entry Point Randomization   Library functions are identified by a standardized set of entry points. The order of these entry points can be randomized as long as all legitimate code using these entry points is updated to use the correct entries afterward. Crane et al. [40] randomized the order of entries in the procedure linkage table (PLT) that is used to call dynamically linked functions on Linux systems. Additionally, dummy entries can be inserted to increase the number of possible permutations; since dummy entries are never used by legitimate code, they can be booby trapped to terminate execution [38]. This breaks return-into-`libc` attacks that rely on the PLT layout.

Virtual Method Table Randomization   The counterfeit object-oriented programming technique [105] summarized in Section 2.1.4 works by chaining C++ virtual method calls together in unintended ways. The target of a C++ virtual method call is determined at runtime by indexing into a virtual method table (vtable). The COOP technique is therefore dependent on the concrete vtable layout of any classes used during the attack. Since the vtable representation is implementation dependent, it can be randomized as long as all virtual method call sites are updated accordingly [40].

3.6 SYSTEM LEVEL

Some transformations are tailored toward system software such as the operating system. *System Call Mapping Randomization,* for instance, is a variant of function parameter diversification that targets the system call interface between processes and the operating system kernel. Without

Table 3.1: Overview of randomizing transformations (1/2)

Study	When	Manual	Equiv. Inst. Subst.	Equiv. Inst. Seq.	Inst. Reordering	Reg. Alloc. Rand.	Garbage Code Ins.	Basic Block Reordering	Opaque Predicate Ins.	Branch/Call Fun. Ins.	Cond. Branch Flipping	Control Flow Flattening	Function Reordering	Function Param. Rand.	Call Graph Rand.	Data Rand.	Syscall. Mapping Rand.	Base Addr. Rand.	Stack Layout Rand.	Lib. Entry Point Rand.	Prog. Encoding Rand.
Randell [100]	A	✓																			
Chen and Avizienis [22]	A	✓																			
Cohen [28]	C		✓*		✓*	✓*	✓*								✓*	✓*					
Forrest et al. [49]	C		✓*	✓*	✓*		✓*	✓*								✓*					✓*
PaX [95]	C, L																	✓			
Chew and Song [26]	C, L																✓		✓	✓	
Bhatkar et al. [10]	I															✓*		✓	✓	✓	
Kc et al. [70]	I																✓				✓
Barrantes et al. [7]	L, E																				✓
Bhatkar et al. [11]	C												✓			✓		✓	✓		
Kil et al. [71]	B												✓			✓		✓	✓		
Bhatkar and Sekar [9]	C															✓					
Jacob et al. [69]	I			✓	✓																
De Sutter et al. [44]	B		✓		✓				✓	✓		✓			✓						
Lin et al. [77]	C									✓		✓				✓					
Williams et al. [125]	L, E													✓							✓

Legend: A...implementation time, C...compilation time, L...load time, B...link time, I...installation time, E...execution time, U...update time.

Table 3.2: Overview of randomizing transformations (2/2)

Study	When	Manual	Equiv. Inst. Subst.	Equiv. Inst. Seq.	Inst. Reordering	Reg. Alloc. Rand.	Garbage Code Ins.	Basic Block Reordering	Opaque Predicate Ins.	Branch/Call Fun. Ins.	Cond. Branch Flipping	Control Flow Flattening	Function Reordering	Function Param. Rand.	Call Graph Rand.	Data Rand.	Syscall. Mapping. Rand.	Base Addr. Rand.	Stack Layout Rand.	Lib. Entry Point Rand.	Prog. Encoding Rand.
Novark and Berger [92]	E															✓					
Jackson et al. [67]	C		✓*	✓*		✓*	✓*						✓*			✓*	✓*	✓*	✓*	✓*	✓*
Wei et al. [124]	E					✓										✓			✓		
Pappas et al. [93]	I		✓		✓	✓															
Hiser et al. [57]	I, E				✓																✓
Giuffrida et al. [53]	C, E						✓	✓					✓			✓			✓		
Wartell et al. [123]	I, L							✓													
Collberg et al. [31]	C								✓			✓		✓	✓	✓					✓
Shioji et al. [112]	L, E														✓						✓
Jackson et al. [68]	C						✓														
Homescu et al. [60]	C						✓	✓	✓		✓										
Coppens et al. [34]	U							✓	✓		✓	✓									
Gupta et al. [56]	I							✓					✓								
Davi et al. [43]	L							✓					✓								
Homescu et al. [59]	E						✓									✓					
Chen et al. [24]	E																		✓		

Legend: A...implementation time, C...compilation time, L...load time, B...link time, I...installation time, E...execution time, U...update time.

knowledge of the proper system call numbers, the effect of any attack is confined to the compromised process. Applications need to be customized before or after they are installed on the host system to use the correct system call mapping.

Tables 3.1 and 3.2 give an overview of the transformations used in the literature. An asterisk next to a checkmark means that the authors presented the transformation without an evaluation. The second column indicates in which stage of the software life cycle diversification takes place (the stages are: implementation, compilation, linking, installation, loading, execution, and updating). Pre-distribution approaches (marked in Figure 3.7) have been evaluated with a wider range of transformations—call graph and function parameter randomization, for instance, have not been evaluated with a post-distribution method. The reason, we believe, is that these transformations require inter-procedural analysis which is readily supported by compilers but hard to support in binary rewriters. We see that most authors combine at least two randomizing transformations or choose to randomize the program encoding itself.

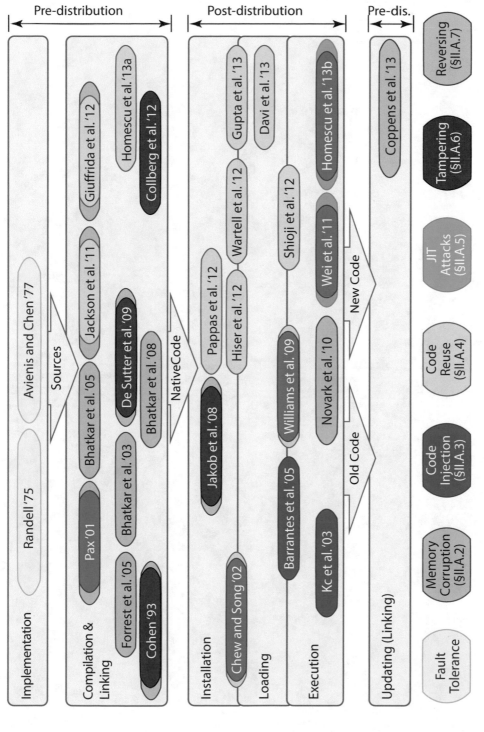

Figure 3.7: Approaches to software diversity in relation to the software life cycle, their inputs, and the attacks they mitigate.

CHAPTER 4

When to Diversify

4.1 THE SOFTWARE LIFE CYCLE

The life cycle of most software follows a similar trajectory: implementation, compilation, linking, installation, loading, executing, and updating. Variations arise because some types of software, typically scripts, are distributed in source form. Figure 3.7 on page 23 shows how the approaches that we survey fit into the software life cycle. Some approaches are staged and therefore span multiple life cycle events; we place these according to the earliest stage. We cover individual diversification techniques according to the software life cycle from the implementation phase to the update phase.

A diversification engine need not randomize the input program it processes. Several approaches defer diversification by making programs *self-randomizing* [10, 11, 53, 57, 123]. Deferred diversification is typically achieved by instrumenting programs to mutate one or more implementation aspects as the program is loaded by the operating system or as it runs.

Instead of installing several programs instrumented to randomize themselves, the diversification functionality can be included in the operating system [26, 95]. This is exactly how ASLR[1] is implemented. A compiler prepares the code for base address randomization by generating position-independent code; the operating system loader and dynamic linker then adjust the virtual memory addresses at which the code is loaded.

Consequently, with deferred diversification, all instances of a program share the same on-disk representation—only the in-memory representations vary. This has several important implications. Deferred approaches remain compatible with current software distribution practices; the program delivered to end users by simply copying the program or program installer. When diversification is deferred, the program vendor avoids the cost of diversifying each program copy. Instead the cost is distributed evenly among end users. The end user systems, however, must be sufficiently powerful to run the diversification engine. While this is not an issue for traditional desktop and laptop systems, the situation is less clear in the mobile and embedded spaces.

Second, when diversification is deferred, an attacker does not improve the odds of a successful attack with knowledge of the on-disk program representation.

However, deferred diversification cannot provide protection from certain attacks. Client-side tampering [31] and patch reverse-engineering [33] remain possible since end users can inspect the program binaries before diversification. Software diversification can also be used for

---

[1] ASLR is an example of a diversification technique that required compiler customization to produce position independent code. All major C/C++ compilers currently support this security feature.

watermarking [46]. If a seed value drives the diversification process and a unique seed is used to produce each program variant, the implementation of each variant is unique, too. If each customer is given a unique program variant, and the seed is linked to the purchase, unauthorized copying of the program binary can be traced back to the original purchase. However, such use of diversity is also hampered by deferred diversification.

Implementation   The idea of software diversity was originally explored as a way to obtain fault-tolerance in mission critical software. Approaches to software fault-tolerance are broadly classified as single-version or multi-version techniques. Early examples of the latter kind include Recovery Blocks [100] and N-Version programming [5] that are based on *design diversity*. The conjecture of design diversity is that components designed and implemented differently, e.g., using separate teams, different programming languages and algorithms, have a very low probability of containing similar errors. When combined with a voting mechanism that selects among the outputs of each component, it is possible to construct a robust system out of faulty components.

Since design diversity is only increased at the expense of additional manpower, these techniques are far too costly to see application outside specialized domains such as aerospace and automotive software. The remaining techniques we will discuss aim to provide increased security, and are fully automatic and thus relevant to a greater range of application domains. This means that diversity is introduced later in the software life cycle by a compiler or binary rewriting system.

Compilation and Linking   Implementing diversity in a compiler makes the process automatic by avoiding changes to the source code of programs. In contrast to humans, compilers do not have a high-level understanding of the input source code and must preserve semantics above all. This limits compile-time diversity (and other fully automated approaches) to program transformations that can be proven to preserve semantics. This generally excludes high-level transformations such as changes to the algorithms that make up a program; as Tables 3.1 and 3.2 show, a plethora of lower-level transformations are possible.

Conceptually, compilers are structured as a sequence of code transformation passes. The major passes include parsing the source code into a compiler intermediate representation (IR), performing machine-independent optimizations on the IR, and finally converting the IR into a lower-level representation to perform machine-dependent optimizations. The machine-dependent passes make up the compiler back-end and include optimizations such as instruction selection, instruction scheduling, and register allocation. The randomizing transformations surveyed in the preceding section are often implemented by adding new pipeline passes; randomized register allocation or randomized function inlining only require a few modifications to the heuristics of existing passes. On the other hand, transformations such as garbage insertion or opaque predicate insertion are often added as new compilation passes. When adding a diversifying transformation, care must be taken to prevent later optimization passes from undoing its effects, e.g., dead-code elimination might unintentionally remove garbage code.

From a software engineering perspective, re-purposing a compiler to perform diversification offers at least four benefits:

1. *Reuse avoids duplication of effort:* Many of the randomizing transformations described in Chapter 3 require data-flow analysis to determine if the randomizing transformation is possible. Since compilers already contain the prerequisite analyses [117], such transformations are easy to support.

2. *Compilers target multiple hardware platforms:* Compilers are highly sophisticated and thus costly to produce and maintain. The high costs are typically amortized by supporting multiple instruction sets in the compiler back-end. The GNU Compiler Collection release 4.8, for example, supports over 50 different hardware models and configurations. Consequently, randomizing transformations can easily target all platforms supported by the host compiler.

3. *Compilation avoids the need for disassembly:* The transformation from source code to object code is a lossy transformation. Optimizations obscure the original program structure and code is interspersed with data. As a result, perfect recovery of the original program control flow is not generally possible [28, 62]. Consequently, disassemblers rely on heuristics that work most of the time. To preserve correctness when these heuristics fail, runtime mechanisms are necessary to detect and recover from disassembly errors.

4. *Compilers support profile guided optimization:* It is well known that many programs spend roughly 90% of their time executing 10% of the code. Most compilers can instrument and execute a program to discover the "hot" code paths. A subsequent compilation pass uses the profile information to better optimize frequently executed code at the expense of less frequently executed code [98]. Since diversification tends to make programs run slower, reducing the amount of diversification for hot code fragments significantly lowers the performance overhead [33, 60].

Unfortunately, it is not always possible to customize a compiler. While two of the major production compilers in use today—the GNU Compiler Collection and LLVM—have open source licenses, several proprietary compilers remain in widespread use. Absent any extension mechanism and vendor support, proprietary compilers cannot act as diversification engines. While customizing a compiler may be the natural way to implement diversification, two alternatives are also available. First, source-to-source transformations can be applied *prior* to compilation. Bhatkar et al. do so to make programs self-randomizing at load time [11]. Second, program diversification can happen *after* compilation in one of two ways. The first way is to instruct the compiler to output assembly code such that it can be rewritten before it is assembled and linked [76]. The second way is to disassemble and rewrite the object files produced by the compiler before or during linking [10]. These link-time diversification techniques have the following advantages:

- *Debugging information is available:* Software vendors typically strip binaries of debug information before they are distributed since debugging information facilitates reverse engineering. So, in contrast to post-link diversification, reliable static disassembly is feasible.

- *The approach is compatible with proprietary compilers and linkers:* Diversification after compilation (and before linking) is possible even on platforms where neither the compiler nor the linker is amenable to customization.

- *Whole program diversification is possible:* Compilers typically process one translation unit, i.e., a source file and the headers it includes, at a time. This gives compilers a limited view of the program, meaning that certain transformations are not possible. Function reordering, for instance, is not practical before all functions have been compiled, i.e., at link time.

Pre-distribution approaches (that do not produce self-randomizing binaries) generally share two drawbacks in contrast to the post-distribution techniques we cover later in this section.

- *Cost of producing program variants:* If programs are diversified before they are distributed to end users, software vendors must purchase the computational resources to generate a program variant for each user. At first, it may seem that if it takes n minutes to compile a program, generating a unique variant for x users takes $n * x$ time which obviously is expensive for popular and complex software. However, Larsen et al. [76] show that much of the work to create each variant is repetitive and can be cached to reduce compilation time by up to 92%.

- *Increased Distribution Costs:* While pre-distribution methods ensure that clients cannot disable diversification, each client must download a separate program variant. This requires changes to the current software distribution channels. Rather than cloning a "golden master" copy, distribution systems must maintain a sufficiently large inventory of program variants such that downloads start without delay. Not all inventory may be used before new program versions are released. These changes will most likely also affect the content distribution networks used for high volume software.

Note that ahead-of-time compiled languages incur both of these costs while just-in-time compiled languages, such as Java and JavaScript, do not (compilation to machine code happens on the clients).

Installation   We now move to approaches where diversification happens during or after program installation on the host system and before it is loaded by the operating system.

The need to disassemble stripped binaries is a major challenge at this stage. As previously mentioned, error-free disassembly without debugging symbols is not generally possible. The compiler intersperses code and data, i.e., by inserting padding between functions and embedding jump tables, constant pools, and program meta-data directly in the instruction stream.

Post-installation and load-time diversification must disassemble program binaries before they run. Typically, a powerful, recursive disassembler such as Hex-Rays IDA Pro is used for this process. A recursive disassembler uses a worklist algorithm to discover code fragments inside a binary. The worklist is initially populated with the program entry point(s); additional code fragments are put on the list by discovering control flow edges by analyzing the calls and branches of each list item. Unfortunately, the problem of determining whether the control flow can reach a particular code location is equivalent to the halting problem and thus undecidable [28, p. 578]. Disassemblers therefore err on the side of not discovering all code [93] or, alternatively, treat all of the code section as instructions even though some bytes are not [57, 122].

In-place diversification is an install-time-only approach that sidesteps the problem of undiscovered control flow [93]. Code sequences reachable from the program entry point are rewritten with other sequences of equal length. Unreachable bytes are left unchanged thus ensuring that the topology of the rewritten binary matches that of its original. In-place rewriting preserves the addresses of every direct and indirect branch target and thereby avoids the need for and cost of runtime checks and dynamic adjustment of branch targets. The approach does have two downsides, however: (i) undiscovered code is not rewritten and thus remains available to attackers and (ii) preserving the topology means that return-into-libc attacks are not thwarted.

Most other post-installation diversification approaches are staged and include actions at multiple steps in the application life cycle. Typically a program is prepared for randomization after it has been installed and is randomized as it is loaded.

Instruction location randomization (ILR) rewrites binaries to use a new program encoding [57]. ILR changes the assumption that, absent any branches, instructions that are laid out sequentially are executed in sequence; instructions are instead relocated to random addresses by disassembling and rewriting programs as they are installed on a host system. A data structure, the *fallthrough* map, contains a set of rewrite rules that map unrandomized instruction locations to randomized ones and to map each randomized instruction location to its successor location. To avoid the need to separate code and data, rewrite rules are generated for all addresses in a program's code section. A process virtual machine, Strata [107], executes the rewritten programs. At runtime, Strata uses the fallthrough map to guide instruction fetch and reassemble code fragments before execution; fragments are cached to reduce the translation overhead.

Binary stirring [123] is also a hybrid approach that disassembles and rewrites binaries as they are installed such that they randomize their own code layout at load time. Rather than using a process virtual machine, randomization is done via a runtime randomizer that is unloaded from the process right before the main application runs. This ensures that the code layout varies from one run to another. Instead of trying to separate data from code, the text segment of the original binary is treated as data and code simultaneously by duplicating it into two memory regions—one which is executable and immutable and one which is non-executable but mutable. One duplicate is left unmodified at its original location and marked non-executable. The other duplicate is randomized and marked executable. Reads of the text segment go to the unmodified duplicate whereas only code in the randomized duplicate is ever executed. All possible indirect control flow targets in the unmodified duplicate are marked via a special byte. A check before each indirect branch in the randomized duplicate checks if the target address is in the unmodified duplicate and redirects execution to the corresponding instruction in the randomized duplicate.

Chew and Song customize each operating system installation to use randomized system call mappings and randomized library entry points [26]. Application programs must therefore be customized to the system environment before they run. Since the goal of rewriting the binaries is to use the correct system call identifiers and library entry points of a particular system, the topology of the binaries does not change. Again, this means that undiscovered control flow is not an issue. However, the problem of undiscovered code implies that rewriting may fail to update all system and library calls.

The drawbacks of static binary rewriting can be summarized as follows:

- *Overheads of runtime checking* Most static rewriting solutions include a runtime mechanism to compensate for static disassembly errors. For instance, undiscovered control flows to addresses in the original program may be dynamically redirected to the corresponding locations in the rewritten program—e.g., by placing trampoline code at the addresses containing indirect branch targets in the original program. The compensation code invariably adds an overhead to the rewritten program, even without diversification, because it increases the working set and instructions executed relative to the original program. Some static binary rewriters omit these compensation mechanisms [43, 93]. Such approaches are unsafe; program semantics may not be preserved due to disassembly errors.

- *Incompatibility with code signing* Commercial binaries use digital signatures, and modern app stores require them. This allows the operating system to establish the provenance of the code and verify its integrity before launching an application. Binary rewriters that change the on-disk representation of programs cause these checks to fail.

- *Heterogeneity of binary program representations* Program binaries do not solely consist of machine code; they also contain various forms of meta-data such as relocation information, dynamic linker structures, exception handling meta-data, debug information, etc. Static binary rewriters must be able to parse this meta-data to discover additional control flow. The format of this meta-data is not only operating system specific—it is also specific to the compiler and linker that generated the binary. So in contrast to compilers, whose input languages are mostly platform agnostic, it requires far more effort to support multiple operating systems and compilers in a binary rewriter.

All post-distribution approaches, e.g., those that diversify software on the end user's system rather than prior to its distribution, share several key advantages and drawbacks. The advantages are:

- *Legacy binaries without source code can be diversified* Since these approaches require no code-producer cooperation, legacy and proprietary software can be diversified without access to the source code.

- *Distribution of a single binary* Post-distribution diversification remains compatible with the current practice of distributing identical binaries to all users.

- *Amortization of diversification costs* Unlike pre-distribution techniques, post-distribution diversification spreads this cost among the entire user base.

The drawbacks are:

- *No protection against client side attacks* Since post-distribution diversification runs on clients, the process can be disabled by malware or the end users themselves. If diversity is used to watermark binaries and raise the cost of reverse engineering and tampering, it must be applied prior to distribution.

- *The diversification engine increases the trusted computing base* Widely distributed software such as the Java Virtual Machine, Adobe Reader, and Flash are valuable to attackers. Since all systems must host a copy of the diversification engine, it becomes another high visibility target.

- *No support for operating system diversification* In contrast, several compile-time diversification approaches support operating system protection [26, 53, 68]. Rewriting kernel code is not impossible but it is rather involved because kernels differ from application code in numerous ways. Kernel code is self-loading and does not adhere to a particular binary format; Linux images, for instance, consist of a small decompression stub and a compressed data-stream. The control flow in kernels is also particularly hard to analyze due to extensive use of hand-written assembly and indirect function calls for modularity. The control flows from system calls, exception handlers, and interrupt handlers are implicit and must be discovered by parsing kernel specific data structures. Additionally, some code cannot be altered or moved since it interacts closely with the underlying hardware.

Loading   Load-time diversification approaches do not change the on-disk representation of programs. Rather, they perform randomization as these are loaded into memory by the operating system.

Many deferred diversification approaches perform randomization at load-time. With ASLR for instance, the compiler prepares binaries for randomization during code generation while the loader selects the randomized base address.

Several load-time diversification approaches also have runtime components. Barrantes et al. [7], for instance, randomizes the instruction set encoding as code is loaded and uses the Valgrind dynamic binary rewriter [88] to decode the original machine instructions as they are about to execute. Williams et al. [125] similarly implement instruction set randomization atop the Strata process virtual machine. Their approach even has a compile-time component to prepare binaries by adding an extra "hidden" parameter to each function. This parameter acts as a per-function key whose expected value is randomly chosen at load-time and checked on each function invocation. The process virtual machine instruments each function to verify that the correct key was supplied;

it also randomizes the instruction set encoding to prevent code injection. Without knowledge of the random key value, function-level code-reuse (e.g., return-into-libc) attacks are defeated. Finally, Shioji et al. [112] implement address-randomization atop the Pin [80] dynamic binary rewriter. A checksum is added to certain bits in each address used in control-flow transfers, and the checksum is checked prior to each such transfer. Attacker injected addresses can be detected due to invalid checksums. Checksums are computed by adding a random value to a subset of the bits in the original address and hashing it.

In contrast to these hybrid approaches, Davi et al. [43] implement a pure load-time diversification approach that randomizes all segments of program binaries. The code is disassembled and split into code fragments at call and branch instructions. The resulting code fragments are used to permute the in-memory layout of the program. The authors assume that binaries contain relocation information to facilitate disassembly and consequently omit a mechanism to compensate for disassembly errors.

In addition to the general benefits of post-distribution, the particular benefits of load-time diversity are:

- *Compatibility with signed binaries* Load-time diversification avoids making changes to the on-disk representation of binaries and therefore permits integrity checking of signed binaries in contrast to post-installation rewriting approaches.

- *Dynamic disassembly* With the exception of Davi et al. [43], load-time approaches are based on dynamic binary rewriting. Rather than trying to recover the complete control flow before execution, the rewriting proceeds on a by-need basis starting from the program entry point. Control flow transfers to code that has not already been processed are intercepted and rewritten before execution; already translated code fragments are stored in a code cache to avoid repeated translation of frequently executed code. This avoids disassembly errors and consequently the need to handle these at runtime.

The drawbacks of load-time approaches are:

- *Runtime overhead of dynamic rewriting* Dynamic rewriting, like dynamic compilation, happens at runtime and thereby adds to the execution time. In addition, the binary rewriter itself, its meta-data, and code cache increase the pressure on the cache hierarchy and the branch predictors.

- *No sharing of code pages for randomized libraries* Operating systems use virtual memory translation to share a single copy of a shared library when it is loaded by multiple processes. Since libraries such as libc are loaded by almost every process on a Unix system, this leads to substantial savings. However, load-time rewriting of shared libraries causes these to diverge among processes which prevents sharing of code pages.

Execution   The preceding sections have already covered approaches with runtime aspects, e.g., those involving dynamic binary rewriting. We now focus on diversification that primarily takes place during execution. The fact that certain techniques, i.e., dynamic memory allocation and dynamic compilation, cannot be randomized before the program runs motivates these approaches. Consequently, runtime diversification approaches complement all previously discussed approaches by randomizing additional program aspects.

Many heap-based exploits rely on the heap layout. Randomizing the placement of dynamically allocated data and meta-data makes such attacks more difficult. The heap layout is randomized one object at a time by modifying the memory allocator [92]. The diversifying allocator has several degrees of freedom. It can lay out objects sparsely and randomly in the virtual address space rather than packing them closely together. It can also fill objects with random data once they are released to neutralize use-after-free bugs.

Dynamic code generation has also been exploited via JIT-spraying attacks against web browsers that compile JavaScript to native code. Like ahead-of-time compilers, just-in-time compilers can be modified to randomize the code they generate [124]. For legacy and proprietary JIT-compilers, dynamic binary rewriting enables randomization without any source code changes at the expense of a higher performance penalty [59]. Such rewriting, however, creates higher overheads than code randomization done directly by the JIT-compiler.

Updating   Program patches are the delivery vehicle for security and usability improvements. Attackers can compute the code changes between two versions by comparing a program before and after applying an update. Unfortunately, knowledge of the code changes helps adversaries locate exploitable bugs and target users that have not yet updated their software.

Software updates can be protected by diversifying each program release before generating the patch. This has two beneficial effects. First, diversification will make the machine code diverge even in places where the source code of the two program releases do not; this potentially hides the "real" changes in a sea of artificial ones. Second, diversification can be done iteratively until the heuristics used to correlate two program versions fail; this greatly increases the required effort to compare two program releases at the binary level [33, 34]. Note that diversity against reverse engineering program updates works by randomizing different program releases (temporal diversity) rather than randomizing program implementations between different systems (spatial diversity).

Software diversity can also be used to introduce artificial software updates. It is generally recognized that, given full access to a binary, a determined adversary can successfully reverse engineer and modify the program given enough time [28]. If the binary requires server access to work, the server can force client systems to download a continuous stream of updates by refusing to work with older client software releases [31]. This exhausts the resources of an adversary since he is forced to reverse engineer each individual release.

4.2   QUANTIFYING THE IMPACT OF DIVERSITY

The preceding section described software diversification approaches in qualitative terms. While this is important to *implementors* of diversification engines, it does not help *adopters* of diversified software quantify the associated costs and benefits. This section survey how researchers quantify the security and performance impacts of software diversity.

4.2.1   SECURITY IMPACT

Software diversity is a broad defense against current and future implementation-dependent attacks. This makes it hard to accurately determine its security properties before it is deployed. The goal of diversity—to drive up costs to attackers—cannot be measured directly, so researchers resort to proxy measurements. Ordered from abstract to concrete, the security evaluation approaches used in the literature are:

Entropy analysis   Entropy is a generic way to measure how unpredictable the implementation of a binary is after diversification. Low entropy solutions, e.g., ASLR on 32-bit systems, are insecure because an attacker can defeat randomization via brute-force attacks [111]. Entropy, however, overestimates the security impact somewhat since two program variants can differ at the implementation level and yet be vulnerable to the same attack.

Attack-specific code analysis   The construction of certain attacks has been partially automated. Gadget scanners [58, 103, 106], for instance, automate the construction of ROP chains. These tools are typically used to show that a code reuse attack generated by scanning an undiversified binary stops working after diversification. However, adversaries could collect a set of diversified binaries and compute their shared attack surface which consists of the gadgets that survive diversification—i.e., they reside at the same location and are functionally equivalent. Homescu et al. [60, 61] use this stricter criterion—surviving gadgets—in their security evaluations. (See next chapter for additional details.)

Logical argument   Early papers on diversity did not qualify the security properties and rely on logical argumentation instead [28]. For instance, if an attack depends on a particular property (say the memory or code layout of an application) which is randomized by design, then the defense must succeed. Unfortunately, such reasoning does not demonstrate the entropy of the solution, i.e., how hard it is for an attacker to guess how a program was randomized.

Testing against concrete attacks   Often, researchers can build or obtain concrete attacks of the type their technique defend against. Showing that such attacks succeed before diversification but fail afterward is a common proxy for security. Again, such testing does not imply high entropy.

Since each of the ways to evaluate security impacts are imperfect, authors often use both abstract and concrete security evaluations. Table 4.1 shows how each implementation evaluates the impact of their approach. One commonality among all evaluations is the assumption that the effects of diversification remain hidden from attackers. However, in Chapter 6 we highlight vulnerabilities that enable implementation disclosure and thereby undermine this assumption.

4.2.2 PERFORMANCE IMPACT

The chance that a security technique sees adoption is arguably inversely proportional to its performance overhead. So far, the only ones that have been widely adopted (ASLR, DEP, and stack canaries) are those with negligible performance impact. For another technique to be adopted at large, its performance impact must be below 5–10% according to Szekeres et al. [115].

Different studies of diversity measure performance cost differently. The most popular benchmark for this is the SPEC CPU benchmark suite, usually the most recent version available (at present, that is SPEC CPU 2006). In cases where SPEC CPU is not available or appropriate as a benchmark, implementations measure the CPU impact on other workloads, such as real-world applications (Apache, Linux command line utilities, the Wine test suite) or other CPU benchmarks. As the implementations of most of the techniques we discussed are not publicly available, we rely on self-reported performance numbers from their authors. Along with the average impact of each implementation on program running time, we also show the effects on memory usage and on-disk binary file size (when reported). Tables 4.2 and 4.3 show the time and space cost of each technique.

For pre-distribution approaches, the overheads generally range from 1 to 11%. For post-distribution methods, the range of reported overheads is greater and typically range from 1% to 250%, indicating that implementations of these approaches must take greater care to keep overheads in check. (Note that Pappas et al. [93] use an unorthodox benchmarking approach and that we consider the approaches by Kc et al. [70] and Shioji et al. [112] to be outliers.) While the benchmarking methodology varies considerably, we conclude that both pre and post-distribution approaches can result in low runtime overheads (Davi et al. [43], Homescu et al. [60]). We also see greater variability in the binary size overheads among post-distribution approaches when compared to pre-distribution approaches; in both cases, the overheads are small to moderate. Some post-distribution approaches also increase runtime memory overheads—between 5% and 37%.

Note that Tables 4.2 and 4.3 exclude ahead-of-time costs associated with diversification. For pre-distribution methods, the software developer or distributor may pay the diversification costs. For post-distribution methods, end users contribute the computing resources to diversify programs during installation, loading, or running. It remains to be seen if on-device diversification is practical on resource- and power-constrained computers such as mobile devices and embedded systems.

Table 4.1: Security impact of transformations

Study	Defends Against	Entropy	Specific	Logical	Attack
Cohen [28]	Many			✓	
Forrest et al. [49]	Stack Buf. Ovf.			✓	✓
PaX [95]	Mem. Corr., Code Inj.			✓	
Chew and Song [26]	Buffer Ovf			✓	
Bhatkar et al. [10]	Many	✓		✓	
Kc et al. [70]	Code Inj.	✓		✓	
Barrantes et al. [7]	Code Inj.	✓	✓	✓	✓
Bhatkar et al. [11]	Many	✓		✓	
Kil et al. [71]	Mem. Corr.	✓	✓	✓	
Bhatkar and Sekar [9]	Mem. Corr.	✓		✓	
De Sutter et al. [44]	Code Matching		✓	✓	
Lin et al. [77]	Many		✓	✓	✓
Williams et al. [125]	Code Inj., Code Reuse	✓		✓	✓
Novark and Berger [92]	Mem. Alloc., Heap Buf. Ovf.	✓		✓	
Jackson et al. [67]	Many			✓	
Wei et al. [124]	Heap Spray, JIT Spray	✓		✓	
Pappas et al. [93]	Code Reuse	✓	✓	✓	✓
Hiser et al. [57]	Code Reuse	✓	✓	✓	✓
Giuffrida et al. [53]	Many	✓		✓	
Wartell et al. [123]	Code Reuse	✓	✓	✓	✓
Collberg et al. [31]	Tampering	✓	✓	✓	✓
Shioji et al. [112]	Code Reuse	✓		✓	✓
Jackson et al. [68]	Code Reuse			✓	
Homescu et al. [60]	Code Reuse		✓	✓	✓
Coppens et al. [34]	Code Matching		✓	✓	✓
Gupta et al. [56]	Code Reuse	✓		✓	✓
Davi et al. [43]	Code Reuse	✓	✓	✓	✓
Homescu et al. [59]	JIT Spray, Code Reuse			✓	
Chen et al. [24]	Many		✓	✓	
Crane et al. [39]	JIT Code Reuse				✓
Crane et al. [40]	COOP, RILC				✓
Braden et al. [16]	JIT Code Reuse				✓

Table 4.2: Costs of transformations (1/2)

Study	Stage	Benchmark	Overhead			Language
			Performance	Code	Memory	
Randell [100]	Impl.		N/A			
Chen and Avizienis [22]	Impl.		N/A			
Cohen [28]	Comp.		N/A			
Forrest et al. [49]	Comp.		N/A			
PaX [95] (Overheads from Payer [96])	Comp., Load	SPEC CPU 2006 32-bit	9%		N/A	(Any)
	Load	SPEC CPU 2006 64-bit	2%		N/A	
Chew and Song [26]	Comp., Load		N/A			C/C++
Bhatkar et al. [10]	Inst.	Linux utils	0%–21%		N/A	C/C++
Kc et al. [70]	Inst.	ftp	33%		N/A	C/C++
		sendmail	1974%			
		fibonacci	28781%			
Barrantes et al. [7]	Load, Exec.	Apache—SPEC web 99	62%		N/A	C/C++
Bhatkar et al. [11]	Comp.	Linux utils, Apache	11%		N/A	C/C++
Kil et al. [71]	Link	SPEC CPU 2000	0%		N/A	C/C++
		LMBench	3.57%			
		Apache	0%			
Bhatkar and Sekar [9]	Comp.	Linux utils	15%		N/A	C/C++
De Sutter et al. [44]	Link	SPEC CPU 2006	5%–10%		N/A	C/C++
Lin et al. [77]	Comp.	patch-2.5.4	-2.0%–1.2%		N/A	C/C++
		bc-1.0.6	-0.8% – 1.1%			
		tidy4aug00	-1.3% – 1.6%			
		ctags-5.7	-1.8% – -0.7%			
		openssh-4.3	-0.9% – 2.7%			
Williams et al. [125]	Load, Exec.	SPEC CPU 2000—ISR	17%		N/A	C/C++
		SPEC CPU 2000—CSD	54%			

Table 4.3: Costs of transformations (2/2)

Study	Stage	Benchmark	Performance	Overhead Code	Memory	Language
Novark and Berger [92]	Exec.	SPEC int 2006 Firefox	20% 5%	N/A	N/A	C/C++
Jackson et al. [67]	Comp.		N/A			C/C++
Wei et al. [124]	Exec.	V8	5%	N/A	N/A	JavaScript
Pappas et al. [93]	Inst.	Wine tests	0%	N/A	N/A	C/C++
Hiser et al. [57]	Inst., Exec.	SPEC CPU 2006	13%–16%	14MB–264MB	14MB–345MB	C/C++
Giuffrida et al. [53]	Comp., Exec.	SPEC CPU 2006 devtools	4.8% 1.6%	N/A		C/C++
Wartell et al. [123]	Inst., Load	SPEC CPU 2000 Linux coreutils	4.6% 0.3%	73%	37%	C/C++
Collberg et al. [31]	Comp.	SPEC CPU 2000	5%–10%	N/A		C/C++
Shioji et al. [112]	Load., Exec.	bzip2	265%–2510%	N/A		C/C++
Jackson et al. [68]	Comp.	SPEC CPU 2006 Apache	5%–10% 11.3%	20%–50%	N/A	C/C++
Homescu et al. [60]	Comp.	SPEC CPU 2006	1%	N/A		C/C++
Coppens et al. [34]	Upd.	SPEC CPU 2000	5%–30%	15%–20%	5%–30%	C/C++
Gupta et al. [56]	Inst.		N/A			C/C++
Davi et al. [43]	Load	SPEC CPU 2006	1.2%–5%	1.76%	5%	C/C++
Homescu et al. [59]	Exec.	V8 HotSpot	250% 15%	N/A		JavaScript Java
Chen et al. [24]	Comp.*	SPEC CPU 2006	0%–200+%	N/A	1.6–195.1MB	C/binary code

CHAPTER 5

Case Study: Compile-time Diversification

In this section we describe our own compile-time diversification engine in sufficient detail. We provide information on implementation details of our transformations. Next, we discuss compile-time diversification scalability and how this affects costs. Finally, we present the results of careful detailed logical evaluation of our system. Using a logical evaluation method proved to be invaluable, as it was instrumental in pinpointing a bug in our implementation.

5.1 SYSTEM DESCRIPTION

5.1.1 INSERTING NOP INSTRUCTIONS

We implement NOP insertion as an LLVM `Pass` in the x86 backend. This `Pass` uses a probability parameter (p_{NOP}) to decide whether to prepend the current instruction with a NOP instruction. The concrete choice of NOP instruction is randomly selected as well. Consequently, there are two sources of randomness in this transformation: both where to insert and what to insert.

Table 5.1 shows a list of possible NOP instructions. First of all, NOP instruction candidates must preserve processor state at all times. Second, we chose these instructions carefully to minimize the likelihood of creating new gadgets. In the case of the two-byte instructions, the second byte decodes to an instruction that an attacker is unlikely to use. For example, the `IN` instruction forces a processor to read from an I/O port. However, this requires the processor to be in privileged mode to work correctly, causing unprivileged software to fault.

Table 5.1: NOP insertion candidate instruction sequences

Instruction	Encoding	Second Byte Decoding
NOP	90	–
MOV ESP, ESP	89 E4	IN
MOV EBP, EBP	89 ED	IN
LEA ESI, [ESI]	8D 36	SS:
LEA EDI, [EDI]	8D 3F	AAS

Inserting NOP instructions has desirable performance and security properties. Performance-wise, inserting NOP instructions has minimal impacts on both space and time. The added instructions do not interfere with the program's working set besides requiring space in instruction memory. NOP instructions do require hardware resources to fetch and decode, but do not add computational effort to the program's original algorithms; some x86 processors even recognize and optimize the execution of certain NOPs. Security-wise, inserting NOP instructions causes displacement of subsequent program code thereby randomizing gadget locations. Finally, inserting NOP instructions breaks gadgets relying on misaligned instructions.

Not All NOP Instructions Are Born Equal   An earlier implementation of NOP insertion also used XCHG instructions operating on the same registers as NOPs. However, during testing we found that using these XCHG instructions resulted in performance overheads of around 60%. We believe this is due to the CPU invoking its locking protocol necessary for compare-and-swap operations that the instruction decoder cannot drop. In consequence, an implementation needs to pay attention to the selection of candidate NOP instructions.

5.1.2   EQUIVALENT INSTRUCTION SUBSTITUTION

Equivalent instruction substitution is similar to peephole optimization in a compiler, except that it does so to randomize the encoding of an existing program. We add this diversifying transformation technique to the LLVM backend by implementing another Pass class. Similar to our NOP insertion pass, we parametrize a concrete object with a probability (p_{Equiv}) to decide whether to substitute an equivalent for a candidate instruction sequence.

In 1993, Cohen described a general methodology to replace instructions with semantically identical sequences of code [28]. For example, we can replace addition of a and b by:

$$a + b \equiv (a - n) + (b + n) \tag{5.1}$$

as long as we carefully avoid arithmetic overflows and underflows. While diversifying at the source code level allows us to perform such substitutions, we consciously decide against this, as replacing a single instruction with a longer sequence adds computational work and might result in undesirable pipeline stalls. These stalls can cause unpredictable and hard to diagnose performance problems. Therefore, our implementation always replaces one instruction with exactly one equivalent. We exploit the equivalence of move and load-effective-address instructions for moving register contents since these are in the top three of frequently substitutable x86 instruction classes [46]. For example, using Intel assembly syntax, we leverage the following equivalence:

$$\text{MOV EAX, EDX} \equiv \text{LEA EAX, [EDX]} \tag{5.2a}$$
$$\text{89 D0} \not\equiv \text{8D 02} \tag{5.2b}$$

With respect to the security implications of equivalent instruction substitution, there is one important observation: if a gadget uses only regular, intentional instructions, equivalent instruction substitution will not result in additional security. However, substitution breaks gadgets that use unintentional instructions because their encoding is different (see Equation 5.2b). In general, the sources of randomness in this technique are the same as our NOP insertion, namely when to replace and with what if multiple replacements are available.

5.1.3   INSTRUCTION SCHEDULING

Compilers perform instruction scheduling by rearranging the order of instructions to decrease pipeline hazards. LLVM uses a list-scheduler [83, 84, 117] in its x86 backend. The scheduler does a topological sorting of data dependencies to decide how to arrange them optimally. This usually involves choosing the best candidate instruction out of the computed list of possible choices. We diversify instruction scheduling by making a random choice instead. Furthermore, we can easily compute a *worst case* instruction schedule, by inverting all computed priorities in the list scheduler's priority list. This worst case schedule is particularly interesting because this helps us to evaluate the worst possible performance impact.

Concerning security, randomizing the instruction schedule has properties similar to the previous technique. If, and only if, the gadget length contains all intentional instructions of a schedule, then rearranging has no effect on the gadget, since instruction scheduling preserves semantics. Due to the impracticality of using large gadgets, we believe this case is infrequent. In all other cases, including unintentional instructions, changing the order of instructions breaks gadgets.

5.2   SCALABILITY OF COMPILE-TIME DIVERSIFICATION

5.2.1   CLOUD-BASED COMPILATION

First, we address the practical question of compiler scalability. To illustrate why scalability matters, consider a naive approach in which each download requires a full compilation and linking step to create a diversified binary. Since large software packages frequently require hours to compile and link, delivering a million diversified binaries would cost a five-digit dollar amount—even at today's affordable cloud computing rates.

We built a system to compile many variants in parallel on top of Amazon's Elastic Compute Cloud, EC2 for short. Our system implements a classic master-slave work distribution model. On the one hand, the master server keeps track of the diversified binaries using a database. On the other hand, the slave instances start up automatically for compiling new diversified binaries. The master keeps track of the number of downloads for each binary and allows the webserver front-end to serve the undistributed binaries first. In addition, the master also manages the quotas for each specific program and version, as well as a priority parameter to set how many instances that queue receives. Our system keeps a repository of undistributed binaries and automatically add more as needed. We upload the completed binaries to Amazon's Simple Storage Service (S3) using the reduced redundancy tier. This allows us to manage costs efficiently, and is no bottleneck, since we can always generate more program variants on demand. Currently, our implementation already builds and distributes diversified Firefox web browser binaries.

Cost-Effective Provisioning   Cost plays a big role in creating enough compiled versions to meet the demand of a large project. As an experiment, we chose to diversify the Firefox browser because it has a complex build system and is in high demand. For instance, there were over 7 million downloads within 24 hours of releasing Firefox 4.

Amazon offers a variety of virtualized servers—"instances" in EC2 parlance—which vary in their computing resources and hourly cost. On-demand instances and reserved instances are billed at a fixed rate. Spot instances, in contrast, are priced based on demand through a bidding process. We report the cost to compile and diversify Firefox using six types of spot instances in Table 5.2 using current prices as of April 22, 2013. The choice of instance matters; for instance, using High-CPU Medium spot instances cost almost half of using X-Large instances. Since demand for Amazon spot instances and Firefox downloads varies, we (conservatively) provision storage resources for a million Firefox variants as a buffer. Again using current prices, choosing the S3 reduced redundancy tier to buffer 38 TB worth of binaries costs $103 per day.

Table 5.2: Comparison of Amazon EC2 spot instances (as of April 22, 2013)

Amazon instance type	One build (Hrs)	Cost per hour	Cost of one million builds
Small	1.19	$0.007	$8,330.00
Medium	0.62	$0.013	$8,060.00
Large	0.37	$0.026	$9,620.00
X-Large	0.26	$0.052	$13,520.00
High-CPU Medium	0.39	$0.018	$7,020.00
High-CPU X-Large	0.18	$0.070	$12,600.00

Optimized Variant Generation   It turns out that there is substantial optimization potential for compiling in the cloud. For example, our compiler-based diversification process requires no changes to the program source code. Therefore, the repeated parsing and optimization of source code is superfluous. Instead, we parse the source code only once and cache the compiler intermediate representation rather than re-creating it for each invocation of the compiler.

In general, the structure of a compiler consists of separate, decomposed phases. A compiler needs to linearize those phases to build an executable. Consequently, the phases themselves need to be composable. The following two observations allow us to devise a compilation strategy meeting our scalability requirements: first, caching the compilation steps preceding our diversifying transformations eliminates much of the redundant work required by the simple approach; second, performing the diversifying transformations as late as possible minimizes the work for

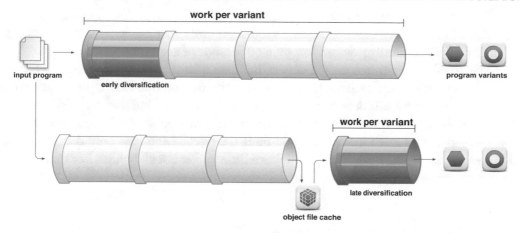

Figure 5.1: Caching the redundant compilation steps as bitcode reduces the computational resources required to diversify binaries.

creating each additional binary (see Figure 5.1). As a result, we restrict ourselves to performing diversifying transformations only in the compiler's backend.

LLVM intermediate representation—bitcode—is fully documented and easy to serialize. The compiler produces bitcode after parsing the source code and performing some high-level optimizations. Serializing the bitcode eliminates a substantial part of the compute-time needed to diversify each binary. However, when LLVM compiles from bitcode, it reruns the language-independent optimizations. This is time wasted since it runs those before it emits bitcode. To get around this we added a flag that skips these optimization steps when compiling from bitcode. This reduces the time to compile Firefox to a diversified binary by 60%. (The compile times reported in Table 5.2 use bitcode caching.)

Even within the backend, we diversify only in the later stages of compilation after lowering of the bitcode into a machine-specific representation. Therefore, we can reduce the compilation time even further by caching machine-specific intermediate code rather than bitcode. Unfortunately, however, LLVM does not currently support serialization of its machine-specific intermediate code. In consequence, we implemented our diversifying passes as transformations on assembly code using the MAO framework [64]. Our preliminary results indicate time reduction by up to 75% relative to naive recompilation.

5.2.2 SCALABILITY IS PRACTICAL

Using LLVM's diagnostic capabilities, we are able to determine that our transformation passes are relatively short, take little time, and that other components dominate LLVM's compilation process.

To determine how the effect scaled, we also tested with a development version of the Chromium browser. We found that on a sequential build that normally averages 85 minutes, a diversified build typically required less than 60 seconds of extra time.

We are also able to reduce the cost of building a large number of variants. One method we used to compile large projects faster was to cache the intermediate representation bitcode. This works well because it does not require any changes to the build system. We simply build a front-end for `clang` (the LLVM compiler frontend) that builds the bitcode for each file if it doesn't already exist. Each successive build finds the bitcode and uses only that to produce the final binary. This means the initial build takes a little longer but all builds after that will compile from bitcode, bypassing parsing and language-independent optimizations.

Table 5.3: Diversified compile time comparison

	Firefox	Apache2
`clang`	21m24.097s	0m52.612s
`clang` caching the bitcode	22m57.277s	1m9.910s
`clang` from cached bitcode	10m58.683s	0m59.858s
Change using bitcode	-49%	+14%

Compiled on an EC2 c1.xlarge (8 cores; 7GiB memory) instance using `make -j16`

From the table (see Table 5.3) we can see that for a large project like Firefox can benefit from this method. However, a smaller project like Apache2 shows worse performance using this method. To look deeper into this issue we modified `make` such that it times each shell command that runs during a build. Table 5.4 shows that C++ files gain a substantial speedup by caching bitcode. However, from Table 5.4 we can see that this method turns out to be slower for C files. Since Apache2 is entirely written in C, it actually experiences a slowdown. This means that the overhead experienced from locating and loading the bitcode is actually greater than simply loading the C file itself. Caching the compilation results later in the compilation process may yield further speedups.

Additionally, `clang` has the capacity to compile from bitcode directly into a binary in one pass via its link-time optimization (LTO) linker plugin. The LLVM LTO plugin includes a compiler backend, which in turn includes our diversifying transformations. Using the LTO plugin removes the need to process intermediate assembly code and object files. In our experiments with SPEC CPU2006, this method saves two-thirds of the time taken by a traditional sequential build. Additional speedups are possible with improvements to the linker and LTO plugin. However, modifications to customized build processes may be needed to use this method, limiting its appeal for large programs. It is also possible to diversify libraries in this manner as well, allowing for statically-linked executables that are fully diversified.

Table 5.4: Average time per-action during make process for Firefox and Apache2

	From Source	From Bitcode	Change
Firefox			
`clang`	0.83sec	0.87sec	+4%
`clang++`	2.77sec	0.68sec	-75%
`libtool clang`	0.33sec	0.36sec	+9%
Apache2			
`clang`	0.37sec	0.49sec	+24%
`clang++`	–	–	–
`libtool clang`	0.84sec	0.95sec	+12%

These results demonstrate that using cloud-based services to build diversified software is practical. Developers and software publishers can use build times for undiversified software as an estimate of how much computing time diversified binaries will require.

5.3   EVALUATING DIVERSIFICATION

We describe how code-reuse attacks owe their existence to the software monoculture. Attackers can more or less conveniently create gadget catalogs from universally identical binaries and craft eminently successful attacks. Diversification by itself, however, does not remove all vulnerabilities. So, directed attacks where the attacker has access to the binary are still a possibility. Undirected attacks, on the other hand, become uneconomical in the presence of diversity (cf. Cohen [28, p. 583]).

5.3.1   ASSESSING DIVERSIFICATION EFFICIENCY

In general, quantifying diversification is an interesting question. Due to its historical roots in cryptography and information theory, the security community traditionally relies on quantification via entropy. While we could certainly follow this tradition and quantify entropy, we think it makes sense to break with this tradition for our specific application of automated software diversity. The reason for our choice is that entropy alone is rather meaningless in our scenario. For example, the entropy introduced by NOP insertion is limited not by machine architecture, i.e., word size, but rather by *practicality*: nothing prevents us from inserting millions of NOP instructions until hard disk size becomes a limiting factor. Contrary to intuition, having a high entropy in this case does not implicate a high security. If we insert any number of NOP instruction in front of an intended gadget, what is frequently referred to as a *NOP sled*, and the attack uses the original address, an attack would still succeed, because the NOP sled does not alter attack functionality. Consequently, we propose an alternative way of quantifying diversification more precisely. It is worth noting that Pappas et al. [93] appear to use a similar quantitative estimate in their evaluation.

Our strategy to quantify successful diversification for Cohen's "some set of attacks" involves the concept of *surviving diversification*. Let us take a look at jump- and return-oriented programming to explain this in sufficient detail. We already know that the attacker's gadget catalog is a list of gadget addresses for a specific binary. Subsequently, the attacker uses these addresses to craft an attack. This relies on the fact that all binaries have identical gadgets at identical addresses. A diversified binary, however, contains displaced or altered gadgets. However, a diversified binary is identical to the original from the point of view of an attacker if both the gadget functionality and addresses used in an attack are identical in both. Put differently, diversification did not neutralize a specific gadget at a specific address, or as we say more colloquially, a gadget *survives* diversification.

The formal explanation follows. Let O be the original binary, D be a diversified binary, E be a function enumerating all offsets in a binary, and G be a function classifying gadgets in a binary at a specific offset. Then we define a gadget catalog as follows:

$$\text{Gadget Catalog}(B) := \{(o, c) \mid o \in E(B) \wedge c \in G(B, o)\} \tag{5.3}$$

We define the set of gadgets surviving diversification as follows:

$$\text{Surviving Gadgets}(O, D) := \text{Gadget Catalog}(O) \cap \text{Gadget Catalog}(D) \tag{5.4}$$

Following this definition, diversification is always successful if the set of surviving gadgets is empty, i.e., the gadget catalogs for O and D have no common elements. However, this is an overly conservative estimation, as an attack certainly needs more than any one gadget to succeed. Therefore, we consider diversification successful if we eliminate most of the gadgets present in the original binary, i.e., if only a small percentage of gadgets survive diversification. We also perform a pairwise comparison of the percentage of gadgets which are common between any two diversified binaries to ensure that there is sufficient entropy in the population of diversified binaries. We describe our algorithm for measuring surviving gadget percentages in Section 5.3.2. Additionally, to better understand the security impact of residual gadgets, we can use a flexible automated gadget scanning tool (such as [58]) to estimate if attacks can be constructed from surviving gadgets.

5.3.2   IMPLEMENTING SURVIVOR

We scan through the .text sections, looking for common instruction sequences—*candidate* matches—ending in free branches such as returns, indirect calls, or jumps (see Algorithm 1). A candidate match is a pair of instruction sequences with identical offsets—one from the original .text section and one from the diversified one. For each candidate, we ensure that both sequences decompile to valid x86 code having no control-flow instructions except a free branch at the end. We then compensate for the effects of our diversifying transformations in a three-step normalization process (see Algorithm 2). First, we conservatively adjust for the effects

Algorithm 1 EnumFreeBranches: enumerate last instruction of all gadgets for original and diversified binaries O, D, and an integer l defining window size; returns a set R of tuples.

$R \leftarrow \emptyset$
$max\_nop\_bytes \leftarrow 2 * l$
for all i in $[0, |B|)$ **do**
    if $B[i]$ starts a free branch fb **then**
        $e_O \leftarrow i + |fb|$
        $e_D \leftarrow$ first position of fb in $D[i : e_O + max\_nop\_bytes]$
        $R \leftarrow R \cup (fb, i, e_O, e_D, O, D)$
    end if
end for
return R

Algorithm 2 SurvivingGadgets: finds gadgets unaffected by diversification, returns a higher-order projection function f computing surviving gadgets.

$validGadget \leftarrow \lambda. S \rightarrow$ valid_x86_instr$(S) \land$ ends_in_fb$(S) \land$
no_cf_before_fb(S)
$normalize \leftarrow \lambda. S \rightarrow$ sort(removeNoOps(leaToMov(S)))
$normEq \leftarrow \lambda. (X, Y) \rightarrow normalize(X) \equiv normalize(Y)$
$f \leftarrow \lambda. (fb, i, e_O, e_D, O, D) \rightarrow$
    if $fb \notin D[i : e_D]$ **then**
        return $\emptyset$
    end if
    $V_O \leftarrow$ filter$(validGadget, \{(j, O[j : e_O]) \mid j \in [max(0, i - l), i)\})$
    $V_D \leftarrow$ filter$(validGadget, \{(j, D[j : e_D]) \mid j \in [max(0, i - l), i)\})$
    return $\{(x, x + |X|) \mid (x, X) \in V_O \land (y, Y) \in V_D \land x = y \land normEq(X, Y)\}$
return f

Algorithm 3 SurvivingFunctions: finds addresses unaffected by diversification; returns a higher-order projection function f computing surviving addresses.

$f \leftarrow \lambda. (x, y) \rightarrow$
    if $x = y$ **then**
        return $(x, 1)$
    end if
    return $\emptyset$
return f

Algorithm 4 `Survivor`: compute surviving gadgets and functions on the original binary O, a diversified binary D. Returns a set tuples indicating identical parts in both binaries.

$S \leftarrow \lambda . (X, Y, E, f) \rightarrow \{f(t) \mid t \in E(X, Y)\}$

$G \leftarrow S(O, D, \texttt{EnumFreeBranches}, \texttt{SurvivingGadgets}())$

$A \leftarrow S(O, D, \texttt{EnumFunAddresses}, \texttt{SurvivingFunctions}())$

$A \leftarrow A \cup S(O, D, \texttt{EnumFunTables}, \texttt{SurvivingFunctions}())$

$T \leftarrow \texttt{HaveTuringCompleteGadgetSet}(G)$

return (G, A, T)

---

of equivalent instruction substitution. Second, we remove all potentially inserted NOP instructions from both instruction sequences. Third, we sort the resulting sequences to compensate for instruction scheduling. Since the sorting step can produce the same result for two semantically different instruction sequences, our algorithm conservatively *overestimates* the actual number of gadgets surviving diversification. Notice that if we want a precise comparison between two instruction sequences, we can capture the semantics of the instruction sequences—for instance using expression trees [106]—and verify whether they have equivalent effects on the processor state. If the normalized instruction sequences are equivalent, the algorithm has identified a potentially surviving gadget.

Automated software diversification only prevents attacks that reuse entire functions, such as return-into-lib(c), if the diversifying compiler displaces the functions. We enumerate each function address, including tables for externally visible functions, and compute which identically named functions share the same location in two binaries (see Algorithm 3).

Using this strategy, we determine how many functionally equivalent gadgets and function entry points remain at the same location in a pair of executables (see Algorithm 4). These two properties are a requirement for a single code-reuse attack like ROP and return-into-lib(c) to work on multiple executables without modification. Because we use `.text` section offsets and not absolute addresses, we are able to perform our analysis in an environment where protections such as address space layout randomization (ASLR) [95] do not interfere with results.

5.4   EVALUATING SECURITY

5.4.1   FREQUENTLY SURVIVING GADGETS

While it is interesting to analyze diversification techniques for their potential of removing gadgets with respect to the original binary, it is necessary to analyze surviving gadgets among the population of diversified binaries, too. The rationale for this is simple: if there are surviving gadgets common among the population of diversified binaries, they form an attack surface.

Therefore, we built 30 diversified versions of all C and C++ programs in SPEC CPU2006 with varying p_{NOP} values. For each binary we compare the surviving gadgets pairwise among all of those 30 binaries with the same p_{NOP} parameter, and record the offset and frequency of matches.

Figure 5.2(a) displays our analysis results for the 433.milc benchmark. We found 433.milc to be representative for other programs of SPEC CPU2006. First, our analysis shows that there is some low-level correlation in the middle of the binaries. This correlation indicates that while using $p_{NOP} = 0.01$ provides a significant amount of potential diversity, we realize little of it as we insert NOPs with only little probability. Therefore, we see that gadgets frequently survive at lower offsets. Since NOP insertion displaces gadgets, we see that this correlation tapers off with increasing p_{NOP} probabilities.

Figure 5.2(a) shows two interesting additional facts. First, gadgets frequently survive at the beginning and at the end of the binaries (cf. Figure5.2(b) and Figure 5.2(c)). Second, diversity at the extremes—i.e., for p_{NOP} at 0.01 and 1—is low. This is to be expected since p_{NOP} at 0.01 is close to zero which creates no diversity.

Upon investigation regarding the surviving gadgets in the beginning and end, we found that this is due to the C runtime setup and finalization procedures. Clang relies on crti.o and crtn.o files to manage the C runtime and links those files verbatim into the executable, *after* compilation. Our first implementation of a diversifying compiler did not process those files at all.

The second issue—low diversity—is primarily due to the probability of insertion. As we have mentioned before, inserting with a low probability leads to only minimal changes. However, the exact same argument holds for $p_{NOP} = 1$, where we always insert a NOP instruction before *every* instruction in the binary. In fact, the only diversity that we see is in the choice of NOP instructions, i.e., using either a one or two byte NOP from Table 5.1. Inserting with a very low or high probability leads to predictable insertions, so we want to insert with some moderate probability. This led us to investigate optimal parameter settings for NOP insertion as detailed in the next section.

5.4.2   DETERMINING OPTIMAL COMPILER PARAMETERS

In the previous section, we found that the probability parameter for NOP insertion shows interesting quirks. Using a low probability, as well as using a high probability result in little diversity. Hence, we determined the optimal parameter for NOP insertion as follows.

We used the largest benchmark of SPEC CPU2006, 483.xalancbmk and built 50 samples with varying p_{NOP} parameters from 0.02 to 1 in 2% increments. In addition, we changed compiler settings to account for function alignment and added a configuration with all diversification techniques combined into the comparison.

Figure 5.3 shows our results of this analysis with smoothed regression curves and confidence intervals. Our results indicate that when using only NOP insertion, $p_{NOP} \approx 0.26$ performs best and loses effectiveness at $p_{NOP} > 0.4$. Also, function alignment appears to consistently help effectiveness: when enabled it disrupts more gadgets. We believe that this is due to function alignment causing more code motion—when a function is moved to another 16-byte offset, following gad-

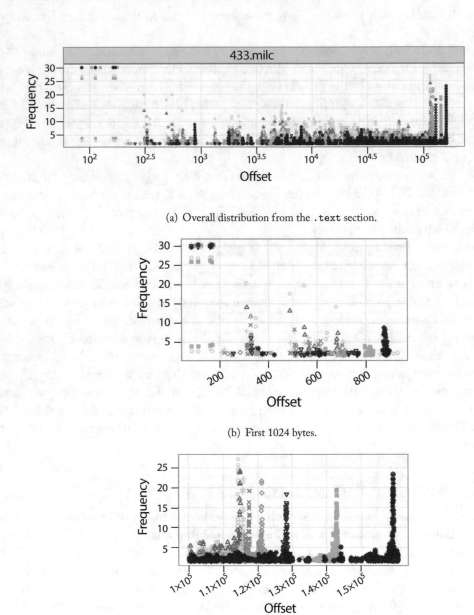

(a) Overall distribution from the `.text` section.

(b) First 1024 bytes.

(c) Last 50,000 bytes.

Figure 5.2: Frequencies of gadgets surviving diversification by location in 433.milc. Colored shapes indicate p_{NOP} setting in percent.

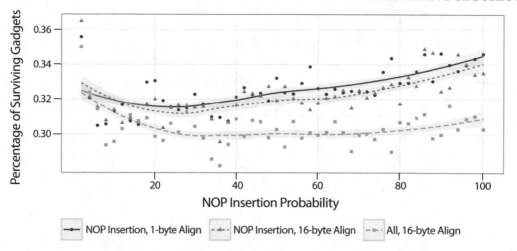

Figure 5.3: Effectiveness of diversification settings after controlling for function alignment.

gets are moved, too. Finally, Figure 5.3 also shows that combining all transformations is effective, with diminishing returns when p_{NOP} and p_{Equiv} are greater than 0.32. Note that we obtained these results for 483.xalancbmk; results from other programs may vary slightly.

CHAPTER 6

Information Leakage Resilience

Ever since the emergence of randomizing defenses such as address space layout randomization, ASLR, attackers have shown great creativity in developing methods to circumvent these protections. Known bypasses rely on one of the following strategies: i) target program aspects unaffected by randomization, ii) repeat probing attack until it succeeds by chance, iii) use information leakage and side-channels to disclose the effects of randomization and customize the attack payload on the fly. The first strategy exploits that defenses, new ones in particular, are not applied uniformly from day one. Thanks to compatibility and performance constraints, software vendors may not apply ASLR to all libraries and executables. Moreover, techniques such as COOP [40, 105] (introduced in Section 2.1.4) do not depend on the code layout which renders layout-oriented transformations ineffective. The second strategy is to probe a web server and other long-running services that respond to requests [13, 111] and automatically restart if the probe caused a crash. By analyzing the response to the request [13] or just the response time [108], adversaries can gradually disclose the memory contents. The third and most powerful strategy is to disclose how the program was randomized by leaking the contents of process or kernel memory [42, 109, 113]. If the length field of an array-like object can be corrupted, for instance, the attacker can use the overflown array to access arbitrary memory locations. Adversaries that can run scripts inside the target application can analyze the memory contents one byte at a time and customize the code reuse payload so it matches the randomized code layout explained in Section 2.1.4. In this chapter, we focus on strategies of the third kind as we believe they are the most challenging.

Information disclosure (or leakage) takes many forms. In some cases, memory corruption can be used to directly read and analyze the diversified memory layout [113]. We call this *direct* information disclosure. In contrast, *indirect* disclosure leverages connections and correlations between attacker-observable memory and unobservable, randomized memory [42, 102]. Figure 6.1 contrasts direct disclosure with pointer-based indirect disclosure. Return addresses saved on the stack, for instance, are correlated with the randomized code layout. Similarly, function pointers in the heap, virtual method tables, dynamic linker structures, etc., disclose the starting addresses of functions. An adversary who can read any such pointer can combine this leak with *a priori* knowledge obtained by inspecting the program offline. If the program is protected by ASLR, for instance, only the base address is unknown at runtime so a single pointer discloses the location of an entire module. If function permutation (also known as address space layout permutation, ASLP [71]) is used in place of ASLR, each disclosed pointer makes an entire function available for code reuse, and so forth. Roglia et al. [102] shows how reading code pointers stored in a data

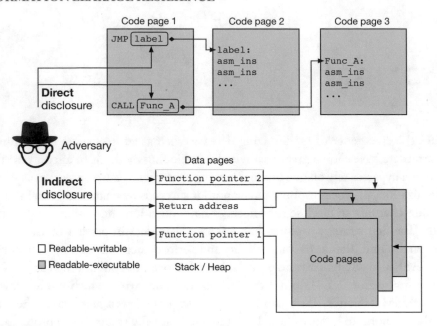

Figure 6.1: Contrasting direct and indirect information disclosure.

structure used for dynamic linking (such as the global offset table, GOT, in Linux) enables ASLR bypasses.

Side-channels provide another avenue of indirect disclosure. Siebert et al. [108] show that, given a memory corruption vulnerability in a web server, maliciously crafted web requests can be correlated with the memory layout. Specifically, each web request corrupts a pointer to a value that serves as a loop counter. Varying the pointer value changes the iteration count and in turn the response time, so the memory layout can be read one byte at a time. Barresi et al. [8] demonstrate that memory de-duplication optimizations that reduce the memory footprint of virtual machines creates timing side channels can leak the randomized base-address of code protected by ASLR.

The research on information leakage resilience builds upon one of the following four ideas to prevent bypasses against diversified code: i) periodic re-randomization, ii) tolerating information leakage, iii) preventing *direct* disclosure, iii) preventing *indirect* disclosure. We discuss the advantages and challenges of each of these ideas in turn.

Periodic Re-randomization The information disclosure stage is a precursor to later stages of an attack. One line of defense is therefore to randomize the program while it is running. The hope is that the leaked information becomes invalid before it can be used by subsequent stages in an attack. Giuffrida et al. [53] demonstrated a technique to periodically re-randomize code and data layout of a running process. Programs are shipped to clients in intermediate form so they can be compiled on the host system. Transitioning from one diversified program variant to another happens by serializing the current execution state, terminating the first variant, launching the second, and finally de-serializing the execution state. Because this re-randomization approach requires significant computational resources, attacks may still have enough time to succeed. Bigelow et al. [12] propose an improved approach, Timely Address Space Randomization, TASR, which only re-randomizes programs when they perform input or output. Specifically, re-randomization is triggered by certain system calls. TASR relies on a set of heuristics and assumptions to find pointers that must be updated after randomization. However, even mature codebases may not follow the C standard strictly and therefore violate many rules and assumptions about pointer usage [27].

Tolerating Code Disclosure Another way to counter information leakage is to tolerate it and instead make the leaked information harder to use. Davi et al. [42] explored this idea with their Isomeron approach that tolerates full disclosure of the code layout. Isomeron keeps two isomers (clones) of all functions in memory; one isomer retains the original program layout while the other is diversified. On each function call, Isomeron randomly determines whether the return instruction should switch execution to the other isomer or keep executing code in the current isomer. Upon each function return, the result of the random trial is retrieved, and if a decision to switch was made, an offset (the distance between the calling function f and its isomer f') is added to the return address. Since the attacker does not know whether return addresses will have an offset added or not, return addresses injected during a ROP attack will no longer be used "as is" so the ROP attack becomes unreliable due to the unpredictable manipulation of injected gadget addresses.

Concurrent with the work of Davi et al., Mohan et al. [82] explored Opaque Control-Flow Integrity, O-CFI, which recasts CFI as a bounds checking problem. O-CFI tolerates code layout disclosure by bounding the target of each indirect control-flow transfer. Since the code layout is randomized at load time using binary stirring [123], the bounds for each indirect jump are randomized and thus unpredictable. The bounds are stored in a small table which is protected from disclosure using x86 segmentation. This forces attackers to guess how to string together a ROP attack without violating any bounds checks; this becomes increasingly difficult as more gadgets are added.

Execute-Only Memory Rather than tolerating disclosure, we can seek to prevent it outright. Direct memory disclosure of the code layout becomes impossible if read accesses are prevented. Thanks to DEP policies, most code is already immutable to prevent code injection. Execute-only memory, XoM, goes one step further and disallows any accesses to code pages other than those relating to instruction fetching. The idea of XoM predates that of diversity and was supported by the MULTICS operating system [35].

Unfortunately, many processors do not support XoM natively. Intel x86 processors launched before 2008 are unable to mark memory as executable and non-readable at the same time. This motivates the eXecute-no-Read, XnR [6], technique which emulates XoM by marking a sliding window of n pages as both readable and executable, while all other pages are marked

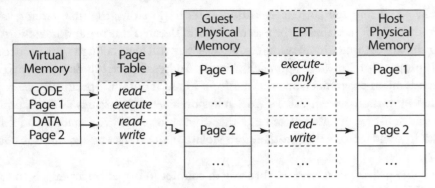

Figure 6.2: Relation between virtual, guest physical, and host physical memory addresses. The regular and extended page tables store the access permissions that are enforced during the address translation.

as *non-present*. While XnR makes direct disclosure harder, attackers can, in certain cases, influence what memory pages are in the sliding window and thus readable. This opens the door to attacks that alternate between moving the sliding window and disclosing the contents of the currently readable code pages. HideM by Gionta et al. [52] also implements execute-only memory. Rather than supporting XoM by unmapping code pages when they are not actively executing, HideM uses split translation lookaside buffers (TLBs) to direct instruction fetches and data reads to different physical memory pages. HideM allows instruction fetches of code but prevents data accesses except white-listed reads of embedded constants. This is the same technique PaX [95] used to implement W⊕X memory before processors supported RX permissions natively. Split-TLB techniques, however, require separate data and instruction TLBs whereas most processors released after 2008 contain unified second-level TLBs.

A third way to enforce execute-only permissions leverages additional page translation functionality that accelerate operating system virtualization. Intel introduced processors with hardware support for virtualization in 2008 [65]. These processors contain a new feature called *Extended Page Tables*,[1] EPT, that adds a second translation step. Previously, x86 processors simply translated virtual addresses to physical addresses. When the virtualization is enabled, *guest* virtual addresses are first translated to *guest* physical addresses; these are then translated to *host* physical addresses as shown in Figure 6.2. The first translation step proceeds similarly to non-virtualized operation so that execute permissions imply read permissions. The page table entry used in the second step allows execute, read, and write permissions to be controlled independently. Because the effective permissions is the intersection of the permissions of the first and second translation step, XoM can be supported natively. Crane et al. [39] built the Readactor system—the most comprehensive XoM solution to date—upon this insight. A thin hypervisor is used to allow non-virtualized software such as browsers and document viewers to benefit from hardware-enforced

---

[1]AMD processors contain a similar feature marketed as *Rapid Virtualization Indexing*.

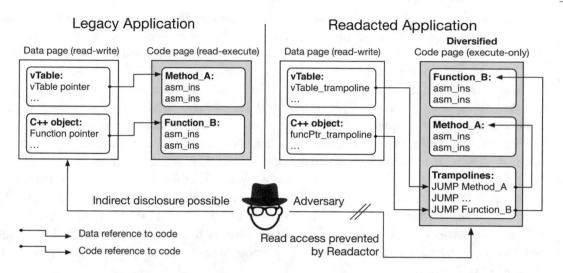

Figure 6.3: Code-pointer hiding relies on trampolines to add an extra level of indirection to pointers stored in attacker observable memory. Because the trampolines are stored in XoM, they cannot be dereferenced to reveal the code layout.

XoM. Because any read accesses to code pages will generate a hardware exception, Readactor-compatible applications should not embed data in code pages. Switch statements, for example, are changed to use a sequence of direct jump rather than an array of data pointers using a modified compiler. All modern browsers generate code dynamically at runtime so the Readactor approach enables XoM-support for just-in-time compiled code too. Specifically, the V8 JavaScript engine used by the Google Chrome browser was patched to separate code and data. Since JavaScript engines periodically optimize and garbage collect JavaScript methods, dynamically generated code is mapped with execute-only permissions when executing and read-write permissions while it is being updated or garbage collected.

At the time of writing, support for hardware-enforced XoM without the need to use the EPT or other virtualization features is forthcoming. Specifically, a feature known as Memory Protection Keys will natively support execute-only permissions for code pages on future Intel processors [66]. While this eliminates the need for a thin hypervisor, compilers and scripting engines still require changes to perform code and data separation. Mobile and embedded systems typically use processors in the ARM or MIPS families that have been carefully optimized for energy-efficient operation. While mobile devices such as smart phones are vulnerable to the same attacks that threaten personal computers, the non-Intel processors that mobile systems typically use may not contain hardware support for execute-only memory. Braden et al. [16] demonstrated an SFI-inspired, pure-software XoM solution that offers the same level of leakage resilience as the Readactor system at comparable overheads without any hardware support.

Pointer Hiding Whereas XoM prevents direct memory disclosure by preventing reads from targeting code pages, it does not prevent pointer-based indirect disclosure. The PointGuard approach by Cowan et al. [37] was the first approach to offer some protection against indirect disclosure by XOR-encrypting pointers with a per-process key. However, PointGuard does not account for the possibility of direct disclosure and therefore makes no attempt at hiding the encryption key. ASLRGuard by Lu et al. [79] improves upon PointGuard by hiding pointers using the vestiges of x86 segmentation with low overhead. Each code pointer is stored at a random index in hidden mapping table. Because the random index is not correlated with the code layout, it does not leak details of the code layout when stored in attacker-observable memory. ASLRGuard only randomizes the base-address of the code segment. Therefore, adversaries can still use the randomized indices to mount code-reuse attacks similar to the "gadget stitching" techniques that enable bypasses of coarse-grained CFI implementations [41, 54]. Rather than preventing direct information disclosure using XoM, ASLRGuard assumes that pointer-less code regions cannot be located by adversaries. However, it may be possible to scan memory pages consecutively rather than using pointers.

Another approach to code-pointer hiding is to use the known concept of trampolines as described by Crane et al. [39]. Their idea is to replace all code pointers with pointers to a set of trampolines stored in execute-only memory. Trampolines to function entries are simply direct jumps but since they cannot be read by adversaries, the starting address of the target function remains hidden. Figure 6.3 illustrates the differences between a traditional program and one using code-pointer hiding. Similar to ASLRGuard's indirection mechanism, code-pointer hiding by itself does not prevent gadget stitching style attacks using disclosed trampolines. To prevent such trampoline-reuse attacks, the Readactor [39] approach also randomizes the instructions at the trampoline destination using register allocation randomization and other transformations that disrupt the data flow between gadgets. So even though adversaries can attempt to reuse gadgets reachable from trampoline pointers, they do not know the effects of executing said gadgets.

Attacks that reuse whole functions, such as COOP and RILC, can still succeed even with XoM and code-pointer hiding in place. Whereas ROP relies on return instructions to transfer control from one gadget to another, COOP uses a so-called *main loop* gadget, which is defined as follows: "A virtual function that iterates over a container [...] of pointers to C++ objects and invokes a virtual function on each of these objects" [105]. In other words, COOP attacks use function pointers in the same way as legitimate programs: to invoke functions, not to disclose function locations. However, COOP attacks depend on knowledge of the virtual method table and RILC attacks require knowledge of the dynamic linker tables, both of which can be randomized and made leakage-resilient using XoM [40].

It remains challenging to construct efficient and leakage-resilient defenses and we expect new information leakage attacks to continually appear. On the other hand, the techniques presented in this chapter all make it increasingly hard to bypass code randomization.

CHAPTER 7

Advanced Topics

While the security and performance implications of diversified software are well understood, several practical concerns remain to be addressed. In addition, existing research has not fully explored the protective qualities of diversified software nor has it reached consensus on how to evaluate the efficacy of software diversity with respect to the attacker workload.

7.1 HYBRID APPROACHES

Unifying Compiler-based and Rewriter-based Diversity A schism exists between proponents of compilation-based diversification and diversification via binary rewriting. It is frequently argued that binary rewriting is preferable to compiler-based methods because the latter require source code access, custom compilers, and changes to current program distribution mechanisms [57, 93, 123, 125]. However, binary rewriting approaches are inherently client-side solutions and therefore cannot defend against tampering or discourage piracy via watermarking [76]. Moreover, a decompiler that produces LLVM compiler intermediate representation [4] can be combined with a compiler-based diversification engine. This results in a hybrid approach where the same randomizing transformations can be applied to source code as well as legacy binaries.

Compiler-Rewriter Cooperation Another hybrid approach of interest is centered around compiler-rewriter cooperation. Static binary rewriting of stripped binaries suffers from incomplete information. The code-data separation problem could be entirely avoided if the compiler (or linker) contains a map of all indirect branch targets; this information is readily available at compile and link-time. Enabling reliable disassembly not only simplifies the implementation of binary rewriters and improves their throughput, but the resulting binaries also run faster without the need to detect and correct disassembly errors at runtime.

Integrating Diverse and Non-Diverse Defenses There are many ways to protect software that does not include diversity. For instance, techniques that retrofit unsafe languages with spatial [85] and temporal [86] protection against memory corruption instantly make obsolete many of the threats addressed by diversity. Unfortunately the costs of these techniques remain prohibitively high.

More efficient integrity mechanisms include software-fault isolation [81, 120], control-flow integrity [2], code-pointer integrity [75], and data execution prevention, DEP. Of these, DEP is already in use and control-flow integrity is entering practice at the time of writing. If the number and variety of known ways to bypass CFI [20, 21, 32, 41, 48, 54, 105] is any indication, this technique by itself will not eliminate the need for strong diversity schemes. Rather than pursuing increasingly fine-grained CFI techniques, for instance, one could pursue hybrid schemes that combine leakage-resilient diversity techniques such as execute-only memory, register allocation, and stack-layout randomization with practical CFI implementations [116]. Finally, one may abandon the all too common one-size-fits-all thinking and instead choose between all available mitigations using criteria such as acceptable time and space overheads as well as the capabilities of the underlying hardware.

7.2   ERROR REPORTS AND PATCHES

Current best practices dictate that program crashes on end-user systems can be reported back to the software developers. The developers use these reports to prioritize and address bugs and to produce software updates that improve the stability and security of their products.

Error reports contain machine state information such as the instruction pointer plus stack and register contents at the time of the crash. The reports are sent to a server that performs two tasks: it uses debug information to determine the source code location of the crash and it matches the new error report with previous reports to rank bugs by frequency.

Unfortunately, software diversity interferes with the processing of error reports. The randomization of the program implementation makes error reports diverge even if two users trigger the exact same error. Programs are typically distributed without debugging information and therefore report crashes using the instruction pointer plus the register and stack contents. Developers store a single copy of the debugging information for each software release to translate locations in the binary into source code locations in a process known as symbolication. With code layout randomization, however, the instruction pointer corresponding to a particular source code line will vary between variants. If not addressed, diversification interferes with symbolication of error reports.

A straw-man solution is to generate or store debug information for each program variant on the error reporting server. Unfortunately, this is space consuming and impractical for client-side diversification approaches. The alternative is to hide the effects of diversification from error reporting frameworks. Error reports can be transformed to a "canonical" version matching what an undiversified copy of the program would report for the same error. This requires a way to integrate with existing error reporting mechanisms and meta-data to drive the transformations.

Bibliography

[1] M. Abadi, M. Budiu, Ú. Erlingsson, and J. Ligatti. Control-flow integrity. In *Proceedings of the 12th ACM Conference on Computer and Communications Security*, CCS '05, pages 340–353, 2005. DOI: 10.1145/1102120.1102165. 10

[2] M. Abadi, M. Budiu, Ú. Erlingsson, and J. Ligatti. Control-flow integrity principles, implementations, and applications. *ACM Transactions on Information System Security*, 13:4:1–4:40, 2009. http://doi.acm.org/10.1145/1609956.1609960. DOI: 10.1145/1609956.1609960. 59

[3] Aleph One. Smashing the Stack for Fun and Profit. *Phrack Magazine*, 7(49), 1996. http://www.phrack.org/issues.html?id=14&issue=49. 5, 6, 7, 8

[4] K. Anand, M. Smithson, K. Elwazeer, A. Kotha, J. Gruen, N. Giles, and R. Barua. A compiler-level intermediate representation based binary analysis and rewriting system. In *Proceedings of the 8th ACM European Conference on Computer Systems*, EuroSys '13, pages 295–308, 2013. DOI: 10.1145/2465351.2465380. 59

[5] A. Avizienis and L. Chen. On the implementation of N-version programming for software fault tolerance during execution. In *Proceedings of the International Computer Software and Applications Conference*, COMPSAC '77, pages 149–155, 1977. 2, 26

[6] M. Backes, T. Holz, B. Kollenda, P. Koppe, S. Nürnberger, and J. Pewny. You can run but you can't read: Preventing disclosure exploits in executable code. In *ACM Conference on Computer and Communications Security*, CCS, 2014. DOI: 10.1145/2660267.2660378. 55

[7] E. Barrantes, D. Ackley, S. Forrest, and D. Stefanović. Randomized instruction set emulation. *ACM Transactions on Information and System Security*, 8(1):3–40, 2005. DOI: 10.1145/1053283.1053286. 18, 20, 31, 36, 37

[8] A. Barresi, K. Razavi, M. Payer, and T. R. Gross. CAIN: Silently breaking ASLR in the cloud. In *USENIX Workshop on Offensive Technologies*, WOOT, 2015. 54

[9] S. Bhatkar and R. Sekar. Data space randomization. In *Proceedings of the Conference on Detection of Intrusions and Malware, and Vulnerability Assessment*, DIMVA '08, pages 1–22, 2008. DOI: 10.1007/978-3-540-70542-0_1. 18, 20, 36, 37

[10] S. Bhatkar, D. DuVarney, and R. Sekar. Address obfuscation: An efficient approach to combat a broad range of memory error exploits. In *USENIX Security Symposium*, SEC '03, pages 105–120, 2003. 18, 19, 20, 25, 27, 36, 37

[11] S. Bhatkar, R. Sekar, and D. DuVarney. Efficient techniques for comprehensive protection from memory error exploits. In *USENIX Security Symposium*, SEC '05, pages 271–286, 2005. 16, 19, 20, 25, 27, 36, 37

[12] D. Bigelow, T. Hobson, R. Rudd, W. Streilein, and H. Okhravi. Timely rerandomization for mitigating memory disclosures. In *ACM Conference on Computer and Communications Security*, CCS, 2015. DOI: 10.1145/2810103.2813691. 3, 55

[13] A. Bittau, A. Belay, A. Mashtizadeh, D. Mazières, and D. Boneh. Hacking blind. In *IEEE Symposium on Security and Privacy*, S&P '14, 2014. DOI: 10.1109/SP.2014.22. 7, 18, 53

[14] D. Blazakis. Interpreter exploitation. In *Proceedings of the 4th USENIX Workshop on Offensive technologies*, WOOT'10, 2010. 9

[15] H. Bojinov, D. Boneh, R. Cannings, and I. Malchev. Address space randomization for mobile devices. In *ACM Conference on Wireless Network Security*, WiSec '11, pages 127–138, 2011. DOI: 10.1145/1998412.1998434. 18

[16] K. Braden, S. Crane, L. Davi, M. Franz, P. Larsen, C. Liebchen, and A.-R. Sadeghi. Leakage-resilient layout randomization for mobile devices. In *Symposium on Network and Distributed System Security*, NDSS, 2016. 14, 18, 36, 57

[17] E. Buchanan, R. Roemer, H. Shacham, and S. Savage. When good instructions go bad: generalizing return-oriented programming to RISC. In *Proceedings of the 15th ACM Conference on Computer and Communications Security*, pages 27–38, 2008. DOI: 10.1145/1455770.1455776. 5

[18] Bulba and Kil3r. Bypassing StackGuard and StackShield. *Phrack Magazine*, Issue 56, 2000. 5

[19] C. Cadar, P. Akritidis, M. Costa, J.-P. Martin, and M. Castro. Data randomization. Technical Report MSR-TR-2008-120, Microsoft Research, September 2008. `http://research.microsoft.com/apps/pubs/default.aspx?id=70626`. 18

[20] N. Carlini and D. Wagner. ROP is still dangerous: Breaking modern defenses. In *USENIX Security Symposium*, SEC '14, 2014. 12, 59

[21] N. Carlini, A. Barresi, M. Payer, D. Wagner, and T. R. Gross. Control-flow bending: On the effectiveness of control-flow integrity. In *USENIX Security Symposium*, SEC '15, 2015. 59

[22] L. Chen and A. Avizienis. N-version programming: A fault-tolerance approach to reliability of software operation. In *Twenty-Fifth International Symposium on Fault-Tolerant Computing, 1995, 'Highlights from Twenty-Five Years'*, FTCS '95, page 113, 1995. DOI: 10.1109/FTCSH.1995.532621. 20, 37

[23] P. Chen, J. Xu, Z. Lin, D. Xu, B. Mao, and P. Liu. A practical approach for adaptive data structure layout randomization. In *Computer Security – ESORICS 2015*, volume 9326 of *Lecture Notes in Computer Science*, pages 69–89. Springer International Publishing, 2015. DOI: 10.1007/978-3-319-24174-6_4. 19

[24] X. Chen, A. Slowinska, D. Andriesse, H. Bos, and C. Giuffrida. Stackarmor: Comprehensive protection from stack-based memory error vulnerabilities for binaries. In *Symposium on Network and Distributed System Security*, NDSS, 2015. DOI: 10.14722/ndss.2015.23248. 16, 21, 36, 38

[25] Y. Cheng, Z. Zhou, Y. Miao, X. Ding, and R. H. Deng. ROPecker: A generic and practical approach for defending against ROP attacks. In *Symposium on Network and Distributed System Security*, 2014. DOI: 10.14722/ndss.2014.23156. 11

[26] M. Chew and D. Song. Mitigating buffer overflows by operating system randomization. Technical Report CMU-CS-02-197, Department of Computer Science, Carnegie Mellon University, 2002. 20, 25, 30, 31, 36, 37

[27] D. Chisnall, C. Rothwell, R. N. M. Watson, J. Woodruff, M. Vadera, S. W. Moore, M. Roe, B. Davis, and P. G. Neumann. Beyond the PDP-11: Architectural support for a memory-safe C abstract machine. In *20th International Conference on Architectural Support for Programming Languages and Operating Systems*, ASPLOS, 2015. DOI: 10.1145/2694344.2694367. 55

[28] F. Cohen. Operating system protection through program evolution. *Computers and Security*, 12(6):565–584, Oct. 1993. DOI: 10.1016/0167-4048(93)90054-9. 2, 13, 15, 19, 20, 27, 29, 33, 34, 36, 37, 40, 45

[29] C. Collberg, C. Thomborson, and D. Low. A taxonomy of obfuscating transformations. Technical Report 148, Department of Computer Science, University of Auckland, New Zealand, 1997. 12, 14

[30] C. Collberg, C. Thomborson, and D. Low. Manufacturing cheap, resilient, and stealthy opaque constructs. In *Proceedings of the 25th ACM SIGPLAN-SIGACT Symposium on Principles of Programming Languages*, POPL '98, pages 184–196, 1998. DOI: 10.1145/268946.268962. 12, 14

[31] C. Collberg, S. Martin, J. Myers, and J. Nagra. Distributed application tamper detection via continuous software updates. In *Proceedings of the 28th Annual Computer Security Applications Conference*, ACSAC '12, pages 319–328, 2012. DOI: 10.1145/2420950.2420997. 10, 17, 21, 25, 33, 36, 38

[32] M. Conti, S. Crane, L. Davi, M. Franz, P. Larsen, C. Liebchen, M. Negro, M. Qunaibit, and A.-R. Sadeghi. Losing control: On the effectiveness of control-flow integrity under stack attacks. In *ACM Conference on Computer and Communications Security*, CCS '15, 2015. DOI: 10.1145/2810103.2813671. 59

[33] B. Coppens, B. De Sutter, and J. Maebe. Feedback-driven binary code diversification. *Transactions on Architecture and Code Optimization*, 9(4), Jan. 2013. DOI: 10.1145/2400682.2400683. 14, 16, 25, 27, 33

[34] B. Coppens, B. De Sutter, and K. De Bosschere. Protecting your software updates. *IEEE Security & Privacy*, 11(2):47–54, 2013. DOI: 10.1109/MSP.2012.113. 10, 21, 33, 36, 38

[35] F. J. Corbató and V. A. Vyssotsky. Introduction and overview of the MULTICS system. In *Proceedings of the November 30–December 1, 1965, Fall Joint Computer Conference, Part I*, AFIPS '65, 1965. DOI: 10.1145/1463891.1463912. 55

[36] C. Cowan, C. Pu, D. Maier, J. Walpole, P. Bakke, D. Beattie, A. Grier, P. Wagle, Q. Zhang, and H. Hinton. StackGuard: Automatic Adaptive Detection and Prevention of Buffer-Overflow Attacks. In *USENIX Security Symposium*, SEC '98, pages 63–78, 1998. 11

[37] C. Cowan, D. Beattie, J. Johansen, and P. Wagle. PointGuard: Protecting Pointers from Buffer Overflow Vulnerabilities. In *USENIX Security Symposium*, SEC '03, pages 91–104, 2003. 58

[38] S. Crane, P. Larsen, S. Brunthaler, and M. Franz. Booby trapping software. In *Proceedings of the 2013 Workshop on New Security Paradigms*, NSPW '13, pages 95–106, 2013. DOI: 10.1145/2535813.2535824. 19

[39] S. Crane, C. Liebchen, A. Homescu, L. Davi, P. Larsen, A.-R. Sadeghi, S. Brunthaler, and M. Franz. Readactor: Practical Code Randomization Resilient to Memory Disclosure. In *IEEE Symposium on Security and Privacy*, 2015. DOI: 10.1109/SP.2015.52. xi, 14, 18, 36, 56, 58

[40] S. Crane, S. Volkaert, F. Schuster, C. Liebchen, P. Larsen, L. Davi, A.-R. Sadeghi, T. Holz, B. D. Sutter, and M. Franz. It's a TRAP: Table randomization and protection against function reuse attacks. In *ACM Conference on Computer and Communications Security*, CCS, 2015. DOI: 10.1145/2810103.2813682. 9, 19, 36, 53, 58

[41] L. Davi, A. Sadeghi, D. Lehmann, and F. Monrose. Stitching the gadgets: On the ineffectiveness of coarse-grained control-flow integrity protection. In *USENIX Security Symposium*, SEC '14, 2014. 12, 58, 59

[42] L. Davi, C. Liebchen, A.-R. Sadeghi, K. Z. Snow, and F. Monrose. Isomeron: Code randomization resilient to (just-in-time) return-oriented programming. In *Symposium on Network and Distributed System Security*, NDSS, 2015. DOI: 10.14722/ndss.2015.23262. 53, 55

[43] L. Davi, A. Dmitrienko, S. Nürnberger, and A.-R. Sadeghi. Gadge me if you can: secure and efficient ad-hoc instruction-level randomization for x86 and ARM. In *Proceedings of the 8th ACM Symposium on Information, Computer and Communications Security*, ASI-ACCS '13, pages 299–310, 2013. DOI: 10.1145/2484313.2484351. 3, 21, 30, 32, 35, 36, 38

[44] B. De Sutter, B. Anckaert, J. Geiregat, D. Chanet, and K. De Bosschere. Instruction set limitation in support of software diversity. In P. Lee and J. Cheon, editors, *Information Security and Cryptology – ICISC '08*, volume 5461 of *Lecture Notes in Computer Science*, pages 152–165. Springer Berlin Heidelberg, 2009. http://dx.doi.org/10.1007/978-3-642-00730-9_10. 10, 20, 36, 37

[45] D. Jang, Z. Tatlock, and S. Lerner. SafeDispatch: Securing C++ virtual calls from memory corruption attacks. In *Symposium on Network and Distributed System Security*, NDSS'14, 2014. http://cseweb.ucsd.edu/~lerner/papers/ndss14.pdf. DOI: 10.14722/ndss.2014.23287. 10

[46] R. El-Khalil and A. D. Keromytis. Hydan: Hiding information in program binaries. In *Proceedings of the 6th International Conference on Information and Communications Security*, ICICS '04, pages 187–199, 2004. DOI: 10.1007/978-3-540-30191-2_15. 13, 26, 40

[47] I. Evans, S. Fingeret, J. Gonzalez, U. Otgonbaatar, T. Tang, H. Shrobe, S. Sidiroglou-Douskos, M. Rinard, and H. Okhravi. Missing the point: On the effectiveness of code pointer integrity. In *IEEE Symposium on Security and Privacy*, S&P '15, 2015. 10

[48] I. Evans, F. Long, U. Otgonbaatar, H. Shrobe, M. Rinard, H. Okhravi, and S. Sidiroglou-Douskos. Control jujutsu: On the weaknesses of fine-grained control flow integrity. In *ACM Conference on Computer and Communications Security*, CCS '15, 2015. DOI: 10.1145/2810103.2813646. 59

[49] S. Forrest, A. Somayaji, and D. Ackley. Building diverse computer systems. In *Proceedings of the Workshop on Hot Topics in Operating Systems*, HotOS '97, pages 67–72, 1997. DOI: 10.1109/HOTOS.1997.595185. 3, 13, 14, 16, 19, 20, 36, 37

[50] M. Franz. E unibus pluram: Massive-scale software diversity as a defense mechanism. In *Proceedings of the 2010 Workshop on New Security Paradigms*, NSPW '10, pages 7–16, 2010. `http://doi.acm.org/10.1145/1900546.1900550`. DOI: 10.1145/1900546.1900550. 3

[51] I. Fratric. ROPGuard: Runtime prevention of return-oriented programming attacks. `http://www.ieee.hr/_download/repository/Ivan_Fratric.pdf`, 2012. 11

[52] J. Gionta, W. Enck, and P. Ning. HideM: Protecting the contents of userspace memory in the face of disclosure vulnerabilities. In *5th ACM Conference on Data and Application Security and Privacy*, CODASPY, 2015. DOI: 10.1145/2699026.2699107. 56

[53] C. Giuffrida, A. Kuijsten, and A. S. Tanenbaum. Enhanced operating system security through efficient and fine-grained address space randomization. In *Proceedings of the 21st USENIX Security Symposium*, SEC '12, pages 475–490, 2012. 3, 19, 21, 25, 31, 36, 38, 54

[54] E. Göktas, E. Athanasopoulos, H. Bos, and G. Portokalidis. Out of control: Overcoming control-flow integrity. In *IEEE Symposium on Security and Privacy*, S&P '14, 2014. DOI: 10.1109/SP.2014.43. 58, 59

[55] E. Göktas, E. Athanasopoulos, M. Polychronakis, H. Bos, and G. Portokalidis. Size does matter: Why using gadget-chain length to prevent code-reuse attacks is hard. In *USENIX Security Symposium*, 2014. 12

[56] A. Gupta, J. Habibi, M. S. Kirkpatrick, and E. Bertino. Marlin: Mitigating Code Reuse Attacks Using Code Randomization. *IEEE Transactions on Dependable and Secure Computing*, 12(3):326–337, 2015. DOI: 10.1109/TDSC.2014.2345384. 21, 36, 38

[57] J. Hiser, A. Nguyen-Tuong, M. Co, M. Hall, and J. W. Davidson. ILR: Where'd my gadgets go? In *Proceedings of the 33rd IEEE Symposium on Security and Privacy*, S&P '12, pages 571–585, 2012. DOI: 10.1109/SP.2012.39. 18, 21, 25, 29, 36, 38, 59

[58] A. Homescu, M. Stewart, P. Larsen, S. Brunthaler, and M. Franz. Microgadgets: Size does matter in Turing-complete return-oriented programming. In *Proceedings of the 6th USENIX Workshop on Offensive Technologies*, WOOT '12, pages 64–76, 2012. 34, 46

[59] A. Homescu, S. Brunthaler, P. Larsen, and M. Franz. librando: Transparent code randomization for just-in-time compilers. In *Proceedings of the 20th ACM Conference on Computer and Communications Security*, CCS'13, pages 993–1004, 2013. DOI: 10.1145/2508859.2516675. 21, 33, 36, 38

[60] A. Homescu, S. Neisius, P. Larsen, S. Brunthaler, and M. Franz. Profile-guided automatic software diversity. In *Proceedings of the 11th IEEE/ACM International Symposium on Code Generation and Optimization*, CGO '13, pages 1–11, 2013. DOI: 10.1109/CGO.2013.6494997. 21, 27, 34, 35, 36, 38

[61] A. Homescu, T. Jackson, S. Crane, S. Brunthaler, P. Larsen, and M. Franz. Large-scale automated software diversity—program evolution redux. *IEEE Transactions on Dependable and Secure Computing*, 2015. DOI: 10.1109/TDSC.2015.2433252. xi, 13, 14, 34

[62] R. N. Horspool and N. Marovac. An approach to the problem of detranslation of computer programs. *Comput. J.*, 23(3):223–229, 1980. DOI: 10.1093/comjnl/23.3.223. 27

[63] R. Hund, T. Holz, and F. Freiling. Return-oriented rootkits: Bypassing kernel code integrity protection mechanisms. In *Proceedings of the 18th USENIX Security Symposium*, pages 383–398, 2009. http://portal.acm.org/citation.cfm?id=1855768.1855792. 5

[64] R. Hundt, E. Raman, M. Thuresson, and N. Vachharajani. MAO - an extensible micro-architectural optimizer. In *CGO*, pages 1–10. IEEE, 2011. DOI: 10.1109/CGO.2011.5764669. 43

[65] Intel. Intel 64 and IA-32 architectures software developer's manual - Chapter 28 VMX support for address translation. http://www.intel.com/content/dam/www/public/us/en/documents/manuals/64-ia-32-architectures-software-developer-manual-325462.pdf, 2015. 56

[66] Intel. Intel 64 and IA-32 architectures software developer's manual - Volume 3 – Chapter 6 paging. http://www.intel.com/content/www/us/en/processors/architectures-software-developer-manuals.html, 2015. 57

[67] T. Jackson, B. Salamat, A. Homescu, K. Manivannan, G. Wagner, A. Gal, S. Brunthaler, C. Wimmer, and M. Franz. Compiler-generated software diversity. In S. Jajodia, A. K. Ghosh, V. Swarup, C. Wang, and X. S. Wang, editors, *Moving Target Defense*, volume 54 of *Advances in Information Security*, pages 77–98. Springer New York, 2011. http://dx.doi.org/10.1007/978-1-4614-0977-9_4. 16, 21, 36, 38

[68] T. Jackson, A. Homescu, S. Crane, P. Larsen, S. Brunthaler, and M. Franz. Diversifying the software stack using randomized NOP insertion. In S. Jajodia, A. K. Ghosh, V. Subrahmanian, V. Swarup, C. Wang, and X. S. Wang, editors, *Moving Target Defense II*, volume 100 of *Advances in Information Security*, pages 151–173. Springer New York, 2013. http://dx.doi.org/10.1007/978-1-4614-5416-8_8. 21, 31, 36, 38

[69] M. Jacob, M. Jakubowski, P. Naldurg, C. Saw, and R. Venkatesan. The superdiversifier: Peephole individualization for software protection. In K. Matsuura and E. Fujisaki, editors, *Advances in Information and Computer Security*, volume 5312 of *Lecture Notes in Computer Science*, pages 100–120. Springer Berlin / Heidelberg, 2008. 13, 20

[70] G. S. Kc, A. D. Keromytis, and V. Prevelakis. Countering code-injection attacks with instruction-set randomization. In *Proceedings of the 10th ACM Conference on Computer and Communications Security*, CCS '03, pages 272–280, 2003. DOI: 10.1145/948109.948146. 18, 20, 35, 36, 37

[71] C. Kil, J. Jun, C. Bookholt, J. Xu, and P. Ning. Address space layout permutation (ASLP): Towards fine-grained randomization of commodity software. In *Proceedings of the 22nd Annual Computer Security Applications Conference*, ACSAC '06, pages 339–348, 2006. DOI: 10.1109/ACSAC.2006.9. 18, 20, 36, 37, 53

[72] V. Kiriansky, D. Bruening, and S. P. Amarasinghe. Secure execution via program shepherding. In *Proceedings of the 11th USENIX Security Symposium*, SEC '02, pages 191–206, 2002. 11

[73] P. C. Kocher. Timing attacks on implementations of diffie-hellman, RSA, DSS, and other systems. Number 1109, pages 104–113. 7

[74] S. Krahmer. x86-64 buffer overflow exploits and the borrowed code chunks exploitation techniques, 2005. http://www.suse.de/~krahmer/no-nx.pdf. 7, 8

[75] V. Kuznetsov, L. Szekeres, M. Payer, G. Candea, R. Sekar, and D. Song. Code-pointer integrity. In *USENIX Symposium on Operating Systems Design and Implementation*, OSDI '14, 2014. 10, 59

[76] P. Larsen, S. Brunthaler, and M. Franz. Security through diversity: Are we there yet? *IEEE Security & Privacy*, 12(2):28–35, 2014. DOI: 10.1109/MSP.2013.129. xi, 27, 28, 59

[77] Z. Lin, R. Riley, and D. Xu. Polymorphing software by randomizing data structure layout. In U. Flegel and D. Bruschi, editors, *Detection of Intrusions and Malware, and Vulnerability Assessment, 6th International Conference, DIMVA 2009, Como, Italy, July 9-10, 2009. Proceedings*, volume 5587 of *Lecture Notes in Computer Science*, pages 107–126. Springer, 2009. http://dx.doi.org/10.1007/978-3-642-02918-9_7. 19, 20, 36, 37

[78] C. Linn and S. K. Debray. Obfuscation of executable code to improve resistance to static disassembly. In *Proceedings of the 10th ACM Conference on Computer and Communications Security*, CCS '03, pages 290–299, 2003. DOI: 10.1145/948109.948149. 14

[79] K. Lu, C. Song, B. Lee, S. P. Chung, T. Kim, and W. Lee. ASLR-guard: Stopping address space leakage for code reuse attacks. In *ACM Conference on Computer and Communications Security*, CCS, 2015. DOI: 10.1145/2810103.2813694. 58

[80] C.-K. Luk, R. Cohn, R. Muth, H. Patil, A. Klauser, G. Lowney, S. Wallace, V. J. Reddi, and K. Hazelwood. Pin: Building customized program analysis tools with dynamic instrumentation. In *Proceedings of the 2005 ACM SIGPLAN Conference on Pro-*

gramming Language Design and Implementation, PLDI '05, pages 190–200, 2005. DOI: 10.1145/1065010.1065034. 32

[81] S. McCamant and G. Morrisett. Evaluating SFI for a CISC architecture. In *Proceedings of the 15th USENIX Security Symposium*, SEC '06, pages 209–224, 2006. http://portal.acm.org/citation.cfm?id=1267336.1267351. 10, 59

[82] V. Mohan, P. Larsen, S. Brunthaler, K. Hamlen, and M. Franz. Opaque control-flow integrity. In *Symposium on Network and Distributed System Security*, NDSS, 2015. DOI: 10.14722/ndss.2015.23271. 3, 14, 55

[83] R. Morgan. *Building an Optimizing Compiler*. Digital Press, 1998. 41

[84] S. Muchnick. *Advanced Compiler Design and Implementation*. Morgan Kaufmann, 1997. 41

[85] S. Nagarakatte, J. Zhao, M. M. Martin, and S. Zdancewic. Softbound: Highly compatible and complete spatial memory safety for c. In *ACM SIGPLAN Conference on Programming Language Design and Implementation*, PLDI '09, 2009. DOI: 10.1145/1543135.1542504. 59

[86] S. Nagarakatte, J. Zhao, M. M. Martin, and S. Zdancewic. CETS: Compiler enforced temporal safety for c. In *ACM SIGPLAN International Symposium on Memory Management*, ISMM '10, 2010. DOI: 10.1145/1837855.1806657. 59

[87] Nergal. The advanced return-into-lib(c) exploits: PaX case study. *Phrack Magazine*, 11 (58), 2001. http://www.phrack.org/issues.html?issue=58&id=4. 3, 5, 7, 8

[88] N. Nethercote and J. Seward. Valgrind: A framework for heavyweight dynamic binary instrumentation. In *ACM SIGPLAN Conference on Programming Language Design and Implementation*, PLDI '07, pages 89–100, 2007. DOI: 10.1145/1250734.1250746. 31

[89] N. Nikiforakis, F. Piessens, and W. Joosen. Heapsentry: Kernel-assisted protection against heap overflows. In *Detection of Intrusions and Malware, and Vulnerability Assessment*, volume 7967 of *Lecture Notes in Computer Science*, pages 177–196. 2013. DOI: 10.1007/978-3-642-39235-1_11. 11

[90] B. Niu and G. Tan. Modular control-flow integrity. In *ACM SIGPLAN Conference on Programming Language Design and Implementation*, PLDI, 2014. DOI: 10.1145/2594291.2594295. 10

[91] B. Niu and G. Tan. RockJIT: Securing just-in-time compilation using modular control-flow integrity. In *Proceedings of the 21st ACM Conference on Computer and Communications Security*, CCS '14, pages 1317–1328, 2014. DOI: 10.1145/2660267.2660281. 11

[92] G. Novark and E. D. Berger. Dieharder: securing the heap. In *Proceedings of the 17th ACM conference on Computer and communications security*, CCS '10, pages 573–584, 2010. DOI: 10.1145/1866307.1866371. 19, 21, 33, 36, 38

[93] V. Pappas, M. Polychronakis, and A. D. Keromytis. Smashing the gadgets: Hindering return-oriented programming using in-place code randomization. In *Proceedings of the 33rd IEEE Symposium on Security and Privacy*, S&P '12, pages 601–615, 2012. DOI: 10.1109/SP.2012.41. 14, 21, 29, 30, 35, 36, 38, 46, 59

[94] V. Pappas, M. Polychronakis, and A. D. Keromytis. Transparent ROP exploit mitigation using indirect branch tracing. In *USENIX Security Symposium*, 2013. 11

[95] *Homepage of The PaX Team*. PaX, 2001. http://pax.grsecurity.net. 2, 8, 11, 18, 20, 25, 36, 37, 48, 56

[96] M. Payer. Too much PIE is bad for performance. Technical report, ETH Zürich, 2012. http://nebelwelt.net/research/publications/tr-pie12/. 37

[97] M. Payer, A. Barresi, and T. Gross. Fine-grained control-flow integrity through binary hardening. In *Detection of Intrusions and Malware, and Vulnerability Assessment*, volume 9148 of *Lecture Notes in Computer Science*, pages 144–164. Springer International Publishing, 2015. DOI: 10.1007/978-3-319-20550-2_8. 11

[98] K. Pettis and R. C. Hansen. Profile guided code positioning. In *ACM SIGPLAN Conference on Programming Language Design and Implementation*, PLDI '90, 1990. DOI: 10.1145/989393.989433. 27

[99] R. Pucella and F. B. Schneider. Independence from obfuscation: A semantic framework for diversity. *Journal of Computer Security*, 18(5):701–749, 2010. DOI: 10.3233/JCS-2009-0379. 12

[100] B. Randell. System structure for software fault tolerance. *SIGPLAN Not.*, 10 (6):437–449, 1975. http://doi.acm.org/10.1145/390016.808467. DOI: 10.1145/390016.808467. 2, 20, 26, 37

[101] R. Roemer, E. Buchanan, H. Shacham, and S. Savage. Return-oriented programming: Systems, languages, and applications. *ACM Transactions in Information and Systems Security*, 15(1):2:1–2:34, Mar. 2012. DOI: 10.1145/2133375.2133377. 7, 8

[102] G. F. Roglia, L. Martignoni, R. Paleari, and D. Bruschi. Surgically returning to randomized lib(c). In *Proceedings of the 25th Annual Computer Security Applications Conference*, 2009. DOI: 10.1109/ACSAC.2009.16. 7, 53

[103] J. Salwan. ROPgadget tool, 2012. http://shell-storm.org/project/ROPgadget/. http://shell-storm.org/project/ROPgadget/. 34

[104] F. Schuster, T. Tendyck, J. Pewny, A. Maaß, M. Steegmanns, M. Contag, and T. Holz. Evaluating the effectiveness of current anti-ROP defenses. In *Symposium on Recent Advances in Intrusion Detection*, 2014. DOI: 10.1007/978-3-319-11379-1_5. 12

[105] F. Schuster, T. Tendyck, C. Liebchen, L. Davi, A.-R. Sadeghi, and T. Holz. Counterfeit Object-oriented Programming: On the Difficulty of Preventing Code Reuse Attacks in C++ Applications. In *IEEE Symposium on Security and Privacy*, S&P, 2015. DOI: 10.1109/SP.2015.51. 5, 9, 19, 53, 58, 59

[106] E. J. Schwartz, T. Avgerinos, and D. Brumley. Q: Exploit hardening made easy. In *Proceedings of the 20th USENIX Security Symposium*, SEC '11, 2011. 34, 48

[107] K. Scott, N. Kumar, S. Velusamy, B. Childers, J. Davidson, and M. Soffa. Retargetable and reconfigurable software dynamic translation. In *Proceedings of the 1st IEEE/ACM International Symposium on Code Generation and Optimization*, CGO '03, pages 36–47, 2003. DOI: 10.1109/CGO.2003.1191531. 29

[108] J. Seibert, H. Okhravi, and E. Söderström. Information leaks without memory disclosures: Remote side channel attacks on diversified code. In *ACM Conference on Computer and Communications Security*, CCS '14, 2014. DOI: 10.1145/2660267.2660309. 7, 53, 54

[109] F. J. Serna. The info leak era on software exploitation. In *Black Hat USA*, 2012. 7, 53

[110] H. Shacham. The geometry of innocent flesh on the bone: Return-into-libc without function calls (on the x86). In *Proceedings of the 14th ACM Conference on Computer and Communications Security*, CCS '07, pages 552–561, 2007. DOI: 10.1145/1315245.1315313. 3

[111] H. Shacham, M. Page, B. Pfaff, E. Goh, N. Modadugu, and D. Boneh. On the effectiveness of address-space randomization. In *Proceedings of the 11th ACM Conference on Computer and Communications Security*, CCS '04, pages 298–307, 2004. DOI: 10.1145/1030083.1030124. 5, 34, 53

[112] E. Shioji, Y. Kawakoya, M. Iwamura, and T. Hariu. Code shredding: byte-granular randomization of program layout for detecting code-reuse attacks. In *Proceedings of the 28th Annual Computer Security Applications Conference*, ACSAC '12, pages 309–318, 2012. DOI: 10.1145/2420950.2420996. 18, 21, 32, 35, 36, 38

[113] K. Z. Snow, F. Monrose, L. Davi, A. Dmitrienko, C. Liebchen, and A.-R. Sadeghi. Just-in-time code reuse: On the effectiveness of fine-grained address space layout randomization. In *Proceedings of the 34th IEEE Symposium on Security and Privacy*, S&P '13, pages 574–588, 2013. DOI: 10.1109/SP.2013.45. 5, 7, 9, 18, 53

[114] R. Strackx, Y. Younan, P. Philippaerts, F. Piessens, S. Lachmund, and T. Walter. Breaking the memory secrecy assumption. In *Proceedings of the Second European Workshop on System Security*, EUROSEC '09, pages 1–8, 2009. DOI: 10.1145/1519144.1519145. 7

[115] L. Szekeres, M. Payer, T. Wei, and D. Song. SoK: eternal war in memory. In *IEEE Symposium on Security and Privacy*, S&P '13, pages 48–62, 2013. DOI: 10.1109/SP.2013.13. 6, 11, 35

[116] C. Tice, T. Roeder, P. Collingbourne, S. Checkoway, Ú. Erlingsson, L. Lozano, and G. Pike. Enforcing forward-edge control-flow integrity in GCC & LLVM. In *USENIX Security Symposium*, 2014. 10, 60

[117] L. Torczon and K. Cooper. *Engineering A Compiler*. Morgan Kaufmann Publishers Inc., San Francisco, CA, USA, 2nd edition, 2011. 14, 27, 41

[118] M. Tran, M. Etheridge, T. Bletsch, X. Jiang, V. W. Freeh, and P. Ning. On the expressiveness of return-into-libc attacks. In *Proceedings of the 14th Interntional Symposium on Recent Advances in Intrusion Detection*, RAID '11, pages 121–141, 2011. DOI: 10.1007/978-3-642-23644-0_7. 8, 9

[119] E. Tromer, D. A. Osvik, and A. Shamir. Efficient cache attacks on AES, and countermeasures. *Journal of Cryptology*, 23(1):37–71, Jan. 2010. 1432-1378. DOI: 10.1007/s00145-009-9049-y. 8

[120] R. Wahbe, S. Lucco, T. E. Anderson, and S. L. Graham. Efficient software-based fault isolation. In *Proceedings of the 14th ACM Symposium on Operating System Principles*, SOSP '93, pages 203–216, 1993. DOI: 10.1145/173668.168635. 10, 59

[121] C. Wang, J. Hill, J. C. Knight, and J. W. Davidson. Protection of software-based survivability mechanisms. In *IEEE Conference on Dependable Systems and Networks*, DSN '01, 2001. DOI: 10.1109/DSN.2001.941405. 15

[122] R. Wartell, V. Mohan, K. W. Hamlen, and Z. Lin. Securing untrusted code via compiler-agnostic binary rewriting. In *Proceedings of the 28nd Annual Computer Security Applications Conference*, ACSAC '12, pages 299–308, 2012. DOI: 10.1145/2420950.2420995. 11, 29

[123] R. Wartell, V. Mohan, K. W. Hamlen, and Z. Lin. Binary stirring: self-randomizing instruction addresses of legacy x86 binary code. In *Proceedings of the 19th ACM Conference on Computer and Communications Security*, CCS '12, pages 157–168, 2012. DOI: 10.1145/2382196.2382216. 3, 14, 18, 21, 25, 29, 36, 38, 55, 59

[124] T. Wei, T. Wang, L. Duan, and J. Luo. INSeRT: Protect dynamic code generation against spraying. In *Proceedings of the 2011 International Conference on Information Science and Technology*, ICIST '11, pages 323–328, 2011. DOI: 10.1109/ICIST.2011.5765261. 21, 33, 36, 38

[125] D. W. Williams, W. Hu, J. W. Davidson, J. Hiser, J. C. Knight, and A. Nguyen-Tuong. Security through diversity: Leveraging virtual machine technology. *IEEE Security & Privacy*, 7(1):26–33, 2009. DOI: 10.1109/MSP.2009.18. 20, 31, 36, 37, 59

[126] Y. Yarom and K. Falkner. FLUSH+RELOAD: A high resolution, low noise, L3 cache side-channel attack. In *USENIX Security Symposium*, SEC '14, 2014. 8

[127] B. Yee, D. Sehr, G. Dardyk, J. B. Chen, R. Muth, T. Ormandy, S. Okasaka, N. Narula, and N. Fullagar. Native client: A sandbox for portable, untrusted x86 native code. In *Proceedings of the 30th IEEE Symposium on Security and Privacy*, S&P '09, pages 79–93, 2009. DOI: 10.1109/SP.2009.25. 10, 11

[128] C. Zhang, T. Wei, Z. Chen, L. Duan, L. Szekeres, S. McCamant, D. Song, and W. Zou. Practical control flow integrity and randomization for binary executables. In *Proceedings of the 34th IEEE Symposium on Security and Privacy*, SP '13, pages 559–573, 2013. DOI: 10.1109/SP.2013.44. 11

[129] M. Zhang and R. Sekar. Control flow integrity for COTS binaries. In *Proceedings of the 22nd USENIX Security Symposium*, SEC '13, pages 337–352, 2013. 11

Authors' Biographies

PER LARSEN

Per Larsen recently decided to try his luck as an entrepreneur and currently leads an information security startup: Immunant, Inc. Previously, he worked four years as a postdoctoral scholar at the University of California, Irvine. He graduated with a Ph.D. from the Technical University of Denmark in 2011. He enjoys caffeinated beverages and staying up very late.

STEFAN BRUNTHALER

Stefan Brunthaler received a Dr.techn. with distinction from TU Vienna in 2011 and spent the next four years as postdoctoral scholar at the University of California, Irvine. Currently, he is a key researcher at SBA Research in Vienna, Austria, working on various topics in language-based security.

LUCAS DAVI

Lucas Davi is a researcher at the Intel Collaborative Research Institute for Secure Computing (ICRI-SC) at Technische Universität Darmstadt, Germany. He received his Ph.D. from Technische Universität Darmstadt, Germany, in computer science, focusing on code-reuse attacks and defenses. His research focuses on exploits such as return-oriented programming (ROP) for diverse processor architectures. He is working on new attack methods and countermeasures against exploits such as control-flow integrity and software diversity.

AHMAD-REZA SADEGHI

Ahmad-Reza Sadeghi is a full professor of Computer Science at Technische Universität Darmstadt, Germany. He is the head of the System Security Lab at the Center for Advanced Security Research Darmstadt (CASED) and the Director of the Intel Collaborative Research Institute for Secure Computing (ICRI-SC) at TU Darmstadt. He holds a Ph.D. in Computer Science from the University of Saarland in Saarbrücken, Germany. Prior to academia, he worked in Research and Development of Telecommunications enterprises, amongst others Ericsson Telecommunications.

MICHAEL FRANZ

Michael Franz is the director of the Secure Systems and Software Laboratory at the University of California, Irvine (UCI). He is a Full Professor of Computer Science in UCI's Donald Bren School of Information and Computer Sciences and a Full Professor of Electrical Engineering and Computer Science (by courtesy) in UCI's Henry Samueli School of Engineering. Prof. Franz was an early pioneer in the areas of mobile code and dynamic compilation. He created an early just-in-time compilation system, contributed to the theory and practice of continuous compilation and optimization, and co-invented the trace compilation technology that eventually became the JavaScript engine in Mozilla's Firefox browser. Franz received a Dr. sc. techn. degree in Computer Science and a Dipl. Informatik-Ing. ETH degree, both from the Swiss Federal Institute of Technology, ETH Zurich.